SHE WON'T MOW THE DAISIES

>>�֍<<

She Won't Mow the Daisies

Stories and Life Secrets from
Minnesota's Northwoods

Leo Wilenius

Thank you!

A most heartfelt thanks to my family who made this book possible. The artwork created by my son, David gives life to the stories. My wife, Lindy and daughter, Beth provided much-needed editing and guidance. Grandchildren (Alex, Addy, Aidan and Andrew) helped design and photograph the book cover. And a special thank you to our forever- nineteen son Patrick for the motivating words he penned as a twelve-year old, "Don't be lame—do something." It's my hope this book qualifies. But much more than these things, it is the sharing of their lives that I offer thanks. In this same spirit, I owe gratitude to the people of the Northland—friends, relatives, neighbors and the community at large. I am fortunate to be part of such a group of characters, and it's their stories, along with mine, that have been a gift to be shared in *She Won't Mow the Daisies.*

CONTENTS

Chapter 2:
Youth
The Learning Curve

Chapter 3: People
Good People for Good Reasons

Chapter 4:
Lessons
What Life is Telling Me

Chapter 5:
Adventures
Merry and Memorable

Chapter 6: Home
Community in Minnesota's North Woods

Chapter 7: Living
Progress and Predicaments

INTRODUCTION

We each have a unique story to tell. My story, I've come to realize, is largely defined by growing up in a remote part of Northern Minnesota near the small town of Cook. It was a protected upbringing and it seemed as if all the people in my young life were kind. People I didn't know, knew me. Neighbors, relatives, neighbors of relatives, relatives of neighbors, police, teachers, local shop keepers - even the mailman, Mervin, felt part of an extended family. And with that, society at large provided a sense of community and a strong desire to get along. What people thought about and what they thought about each other was important. Respect was a common thread. It's possible also that a life growing up with few distractions offered a unique sense of my surroundings. I could be wrong. But that's my story shared in *She Won't Mow the Daisies*—a life where getting along was important, a life in the outdoors, experiences that relate and people who remind us of the good in this world. These stories appeared in the Cook News Herald beginning in 2017 through 2018 but are chaptered here by theme. The memories are as accurate and honest as my memory allows and the commentaries are just my opinions of course. And those could change. At least I hope so. There is so much more to learn.

-Leo

CHAPTER 1:
A MIXED STRINGER

Cats, Comets, & Cucumbers

Friends?

Our family always had a cat as I was growing up, as did most other folks in our neighborhood. It was almost automatic—one cat and one dog. Back when small farms such as ours dominated the countryside, cats were extremely useful in keeping damaging rodent populations in check on properties which, in turn, provided convenient housing. It made perfect sense. Today, it's more difficult to make the "useful" argument. Moreover, cats are a considerable responsibility, not to mention expense, so it's curious to me why they're still so popular. I'm rather practical, so I Googled it to find out why this is. The first answer in line to the question said, "People own cats because they make great friends." Friends? Well, I need to think about that for a bit.

We have a cat, which is still something of a surprise to me because a while back our cat of many years passed away and my wife and I agreed we wouldn't seek another. Then life happened and somehow a lost black-and-white kitten worked its way into our home. The cat had a hunting mentality from the start, cautiously stalking about the house in search of game to eat or grandchildren to terrorize, so when we asked the grandkids to give it a name, "Zippy" didn't exactly fit the profile. But then, they named their dog "Hulk"—a

four-pound ball of fur that looks like a dust mop with toes—
so we weren't that surprised. The name stuck. And just as
algae slime grows slowly and imperceptibly on wet rocks,
Zippy has grown on us and has become a legitimate part of
the family.

Zippy has a few bad habits though. First of all, she ig-
nores commands, which is likely the reason you see so few
cats in the military. She is compelled by her heritage to attack
Hulk, the mop dog, when he comes to visit, but fortunately
she can't catch him. We keep our bedroom door shut at night
because if left open, she's soon resting at my throat. This may
induce an "Ah, ain't that sweet" from some, but to me it feels
like a not-so-subtle throwback to her ancestors' habit of taking zebra down by the neck, which distracts from my sleep.
And while our door is shut, she assumes sole command of
the "Serengeti plain" of our living room, loaded with juicy
furniture which she attacks at random through the night and
up until about 6:00 a.m., which is when she begins to cry for
breakfast. While I'm sitting on the couch watching the news,
Zippy likes to play with my feet until she decides playtime
is over and it's time again to find out just who's in charge.
Call it rough play, my feet and her teeth give it a go for a few
minutes until either Zippy retreats to a neutral corner or my
feet retire out of her reach. And it's not a bad habit, but Zippy continues to gain weight regardless of the various diets
we've attempted, which leads me to believe either furniture is
high in calories or lurking, lingering and loitering don't burn
enough calories.

It's long been my thought that many people have a cat
only because they've always had one—old habits die hard,
after all. But going back to the assumption noted at the beginning that we choose cats because "they make great friends,"
maybe the notion isn't so crazy and maybe it even has merit.

Thinking about my human friends, there are those who don't listen, those who cry about things, those who tend to lurk, linger and loiter, those who are not necessarily useful and those who like to be in charge. Truth be told, I might have a few quirks myself. In the end, a "friend" takes on odd shapes, and that's okay, so I'll conclude that maybe, perhaps, Zippy is my f-f-friend. But for the record, I'm still the one in charge at our home—between me and Zippy, anyway.

Mr. Clean

My mother spoiled me. She cooked great meals, baked special treats, knitted warm gloves, kept a garden, picked up around the yard, did the wash, hung clothes to dry and folded them neatly. All I was responsible for around the house was cleaning my room and that effort didn't win me any awards. Then I got married.

Let's just say my wife was not impressed by my take on "sharing the load" in our new home. Eventually, I learned that washing the dishes, vacuuming or cooking a meal without being asked to do so was important and it even felt good. After decades of progress, one would think that I'd have a good handle on this kind of stuff. But I am also my father's son. My dad (who was also spoiled by my mother), in one of the few times he had to care for me all by himself, cooked

Gaines Burgers (dog food shaped like hamburger patties) for my lunch. Upon returning home, Mom thought that was hilarious. My sister probably thought, *Sweet justice at last!* I thought the burgers were dry. Anyway, at least he tried to help, and like my father, there are times I've tried to be helpful too. Like with my leaf blower.

I came to know about leaf blowers late in life, but what a tool! My handheld hurricane will drive leaves from the gardens, blast snow off the deck and clean the garage floor in seconds. So, one day while my wife was visiting relatives, I figured I would bring this efficiency to bear in the tedious task of dusting the house. It worked well (if dusting is defined as moving dust from one place to another). The problem was that a leaf blower in the house is like the proverbial bull in a china shop. In addition to china, all kinds of things started flying around—doilies, drapes, flowers, flower pots, pictures, rugs, remote controls and the cat. Well, the cat wasn't literally flying, but you can pretty much guess how a cat reacts to a leaf blower. Anyway, I thought I had cleaned up the mess pretty well, but it wasn't long after my wife got home before she asked, "Why, sweetheart, are the teapot, counter top, stove and faucet covered in dust?" We discussed it at length and agreed that the leaf blower was maybe a bad idea. Still, I believe it was a noble effort, because as the saying goes, "nothing ventured, nothing gained," not to mention I like to take "the road less traveled." Go big or go home, I always say.

Then there was the time I cleaned our bedroom closet, again, while my wife was away. Our home is small, which makes for a master bedroom with an undersized closet. I analyzed my wardrobe to see what could be thrown or given away to make room and then did the same for shoes, only I included all the shoes—mine and hers. In perhaps the most explosive thing I have ever done, I threw away a pair of my wife's shoes that looked, well, dusty if nothing else, but they were actually new shoes. If a "1" is a firecracker and "10" is the volcanic eruption of Mount Saint Helens in 1980, my wife's reaction to my clutter reduction program rated a "9." Oops. We didn't have to discuss whether or not that was a bad idea because that was clear from her initial explosion, and to this day we avoid talking about it. At times, I think it would be fun to call her Helen just to make light of the elephant in the room in our marital history, but as they say, "don't kick a sleeping dog," or "it is better to leave the battle and live to fight another day," or "what were you thinking, you inconsiderate slob?"

Most recently, while home alone I decided to clean the wood floors in our kitchen, dining and living rooms. Taking to my hands and knees, I dutifully applied lemon Pledge furniture polish until the entire floor looked shiny and new. Upon returning home, my wife immediately took notice and informed me that I should have used the floor cleaner and not furniture polish because the floor was now as slippery as it was shiny. Even I suspected that was not the effect we were looking for. On a positive note, nobody broke any bones while the floor served as an ice rink and the grandkids had a great time sliding around the house when they came to visit.

Fortunately for me, my wife has grown accustomed to my good intentions and she actually had something of a laugh over the polished floor. In my defense, I didn't know that there was a can of wood floor cleaner next to the Pledge, because those things are kept under the sink and it's very cluttered down there. The space really needs a cleaning. I suppose it would be helpful if I were to do that, but I figure it is better to "leave them laughing" and "quit while I'm still ahead;" that is, if I am ahead at all.

If you need me for anything, I'll be in the garage—fixing.

Looking Up

A favorite family activity is to turn off the cabin lights, then lay out on the lawn on a warm summer evening to gaze at the sky. We bring only the basics—blankets, pillows, bug spray, chips, dip, the dog, and flashlights to find out where the dip and the dog went. There's a lot to look at if you take the time. We spot falling stars, satellites, airplanes, the Big Dipper and occasionally, northern lights. The session usually ends when the grandkids begin to doze off or when they decide it is time for a wrestling match. It's a good time as long as you don't get caught in an octopus hold.

But it's winter now, so why bring it up? Well, cold, clear nights offer great opportunities for sky watching, too, only the gear changes—less dip and more snowmobile gear is a good start. I also happen to be reading an interesting book that has inspired me to know more about our universe. My knowledge of what is going on up there was limited prior to reading the book. I could name the planets, find the Big Dipper and I knew that the tail we see on Halley's Comet was due to volatile compounds that begin to sublime from the surface of its nucleus due to heat from proximity to the sun. Ahem. Anyway, it's a good book, and it is titled A Short History of Nearly Everything, by bestselling author Bill Bryson, who is not to be confused with avid camper/canoeist and Lake Vermilion resident Bill Bryson. In addition to outer space, the book covers the elements, the microscopic world, continental shifts and more. The information is even entertaining because the author chews it down to a form that's easier to comprehend.

Even with this glowing review of the book, I've been around long enough to know that several of you (maybe more) will not read it, and that's okay. But if you're curious, here is just one small bit of information from thousands: Space is big. Even though Pluto is nearly five billion miles away, it's like the neighbor across the street because the known universe is billions of trillions of miles across. And you'd better pack a lunch for a trip to Pluto, as it takes twelve years traveling at 35,000 miles per hour to get there. And did you know that the telescopes that allow us to see Pluto and far beyond also allow us to witness the lighting of a match on the surface of the moon? That's pretty cool stuff, especially if, for example, the Bill Bryson of Lake Vermilion were up there trying to start a campfire.

Outhouse—To Be or Not To Be

Two score past, an exchange had I with a workmate, an engineer some had deemed old fashioned, nay, ancient, for it be he who argued often that mankind is losing focus—our traditions torn asunder, asunder indeed.

Longingly, he treasured the rhythm of bygone days whereupon honest toil, cultured prose and simplicity grounded in the practical ruled over change for the sake of change. Said he with conviction, "Progress is but the politic of opinion." His defense: that we've come hence to treasure most those dwellings wherein sanitation previously provided by remote facilities (outhouses) and applied activities therein have been moved indoors while holding likewise the promotion of space (decks and patios) for the purpose of dining and entertaining outdoors. He posed, "Has not the experience of centuries been twisted?" Not convinced, but unprepared to counter, I concurred with the gent lest he riddle me low. But having considered his points hither, be it with respect to his memory and the trite practices of yesterday, I offer quarrel to the contrary, such as to propagate indoor plumbing for the eons, and shall henceforth cease speaking like I'm from the sixteenth century or thereabouts.

Yes, the outhouse is something of a trusty old friend for many and my former coworker made a good point. Alone on the throne with your thoughts in the great outdoors has some advantages. But therein lies a problem: the outdoors, where outhouses are, also happens to be where a lot of critters in the northland want to be.

One incident of this is a story told by my friend Bruce (Judy) Anderson, a summer resident of Lake Vermilion. Years back, he built a spacious two-hole outhouse for his mother while he and his family stayed at her cabin on Vermilion. Mom happened to have a problem with black bears getting into her garbage, so she took the liberty of moving the garbage can into one side of the spacious new outhouse. This solved the problem of bears getting into the garbage, but it created a new problem of bears wanting to get into the outhouse. Bruce's daughter Karen would find this out while occupying the privy in the middle of the night. Now if that isn't a nightmare, I don't know what is. In a similar case a few years ago, a lake neighbor, another Karen, was kept safe inside her outhouse while a deranged fisher, three feet of muscles, teeth and temper, worked feverishly to get in despite her desperate calls for help. There's nothing worse than an angry fisher waiting outside your outhouse door to go next. And you know full well the longer you make him wait, the madder he's going to get!

My particular gripe with outhouses is that they are a favorite hideout for the biggest, hairiest spiders you'll find in the northland, and it bothers me to no end when one scurries to the "safety" of the hole when the outhouse door opens. It just takes away any chance for relaxation, the way I see it. Even more concerning, I recently discovered a red squirrel living in the pit of the outhouse at our hunting cabin. I'm not sure how it gets by down there and I don't intend to make an investigation of it either. All I know is that red squirrels have a very particular food preference that cannot be taken lightly. Since fishers eat squirrels, I suppose I could put one of them in there, but then eventually I'd need a bear to get the fisher out, and I think we've already established that bears in the outhouse is not a good idea. We'll deal with the squirrel.

I recently read the book *Shakespeare* which noted Shakespeare's plays sometimes drew two thousand or more people to his theatre, located just outside the gates of London, and these productions could last for hours. Surviving documentation shows there were no sanitary facilities in the theatre, or provisions otherwise to serve those attending. Sounds nasty, but such practice was not uncommon for the time. On the bright side, with that many folks running to the woods for relief there would have been little chance of running into a bear because, let's face it, even bears can only take so much.

To future commodes, thus say I candid, "Onward Kohler! Onward Delta! Onward American Standard!"

Eating Disorders

I've been researching how various foods can affect health and conditions involving pain because I have more pain nowadays and as you might expect, there's a wealth of information to be had. For example, I learned coffee is now good for us. Studies show coffee drinkers have a 64% better chance of living beyond average life expectancy than those who drink no coffee. When I was young, coffee would stunt your growth, or so it was thought. After coffee, the picture gets complicated, especially with the "help" of those who will take simple facts and twist them into health theories and money-making schemes. So, if I actually get the nerve to eat healthy someday, I don't know who to believe. I'll tell you some of what I found.

There is much said about lactose in dairy products, which causes an upset stomach for some. One popular idea is that it's not natural for humans to eat dairy products after weaning because no other mammals do. An opposing theory is that milk simply wasn't available to early humans or other mammals after weaning, as neither were foot-long hot dogs or caramel rolls. There's nothing unnatural about it; it's merely another food we adapted to at a later date. I'm currently a dedicated member of the dairy-loving American public that, according to the Dairy Council, consumes around fifteen pounds of lactose-laden ice cream per capita annually, and I dare anyone to suggest that a maple nut ice cream cone from Moosebirds ice cream shop is evil.

Have you heard of lectins? They're proteins found in many foods and one "expert" says they lead to body aches, fatigue and stomach problems. Eureka! And he'll sell you something at seventy-five dollars a jar that will help combat that, unless of course you simply refuse to eat lectins anymore. That's not easy to do. Foods containing lectins include beans of any kind, all grains, potatoes, rice, peppers and tomatoes for a start. Even lentils. Fruit gets a good grade from all responsible resources but again, if you want to understand the twist some marketing gurus will put on it—fruit contains sugar, sugar makes acids, acids can cause cancer, and fruit therefore is unhealthy, unless of course, you buy the miracle "anti-venom" for seventy-five dollars a jar.

Of course, we all know that meat will kill you. I'm just one of the lucky ones whose ancestors were able to pass on their genes before succumbing to deadly meat. It's important to note that you still need protein and fats in your diet if you want to stay alive, some of which can be gained from peanuts, but those can be deadly, too, if you have allergies. Thinking ahead to supper, a medium-rare center cut of cabbage is hardly a substitute for a ribeye or pork chop. I just haven't figured out why meat tastes great but is considered toxic by some while Brussels sprouts are healthy but make babies gag—a natural involuntary reaction that protects them from foods that might be harmful. I have yet to check what the internet has to say about chocolate cake, as I don't think I'm ready for the answer and it happens to be my favorite food group.

Apparently, doctors and nutritionists don't surf the internet much since they avoid labeling foods as "good" or "bad," but rather, all they want to talk about is moderation, exercise and good choices—boring. And they won't give me a list of foods that will kill me or a list of foods that will allow me to live to 104 like Harry Enzmann, a former Cook-area dairy farmer who's now retired. I don't know of anyone who enjoyed fishing more than Harry, so he probably eats fish. Fish is one of the few foods that most folks on the internet consider healthy. Come to think of it, nobody enjoys drinking coffee more than Harry, either, so his diet must be fish and coffee. Did I mention he is 104?

All this information from the internet has me thinking that the ultimate weapon in modern frontline warfare would be to catapult pepperoni pizzas over enemy lines. But that's so lethal with all that protein, lactose and lectin-filled tomato sauce it could be considered a war crime. Maybe just sending over baked beans would be deadly enough. It'd be good for a few laughs, if nothing else.

There's just so much to remember. Eating shouldn't be that difficult. I'd like to think that fishing all day with a big Thermos of coffee is the key to a long, healthy life, but I suspect health professionals are on to something with moderation even if it is rather boring.

Wilderness Man

Dry snow squawks in cadence with each step of his snow-shoes, like the strings of a violin. Bone-chilling emptiness fills the forest, interrupted only by an occasional CRACK from freezing sap bursting under the bark of unfortunate hard-woods nearby. The trap line has been brutal this year. Numb fingers, deep powder and heavy pelts challenge each step in turn. Now ominous tracks stitch the fresh snow along his way. *What lies ahead?* he ponders as he picks up the pace toward his spike camp on the Littlefork. Soon evening falls, revealing a small glow nestled in a glade—the embers of a dying fire that flicker at his form, hidden snug beneath layers of thick fur.

Clear and low, a howl pierces this still darkness, followed by a pitched explosion of barks and growls that fill the glade. This pack is powerful and disturbed by the intrusion of this lone traveler on their hunting grounds. He's heard it before, yet it shakes him still, for the threat is as large as the chance for encounter is small. *Stay awake. They are close,* he thinks as he touches the musket near his head and knife at his side.

But the urge to rest will not wait and vigilance gives way to deep, desperate sleep. It is the renewal that is lifeblood to setting cold steel, traversing that not traversed and maintaining one's wits lest he become food stock for a wilderness most eager to accept it. The hours pass when, slowly and imperceptibly, yellow rays begin to creep across the ridge and a clear morn again finds him master of his surroundings. Strong and aware, the light shows to invisible eyes that he is without fear, and lesser creatures best take notice. His goal for this day, as in the words of Thoreau: to do well and provide a life that is full, if not plentiful.

It is the march of a thousand thousands, the push and pull of living things that challenges man to endure hardship in the north. It is a path shared with the Native peoples, explorers and few competent others. Nature christens these trials neither grand nor dramatic. There are no heroes or villains here, rather a world that acknowledges little more than another day. A day of hope and a simplicity that is honorable. And it is enough.

Raspberry Pancakes and Blueberry Pie

A friend tells me you're not lost as long as you can still see your truck. Well, I won't challenge his wisdom, but during August in northern Minnesota, if you can still see your truck you may not be lost but you're not exactly the explorer of the month either. However, for those folks who do leave the safety of a truck, cabin or hiking trail to get into the wilderness, getting lost can and does happen. And getting lost is serious business.

Survival experts recommend we be prepared in the event of getting lost, but if we were prepared we wouldn't get lost in the first place, would we? I've been lost on two occasions, which doesn't qualify me as an expert on survival, but the least I can do is to expand the menu for those who someday find themselves lost by sharing two "survival food" recipes with you that feature the Northland's finest fruits—raspberries and blueberries. After all, one reason some folks get lost in the first place is because they're out looking for raspberries and blueberries.

The recipes are easy, which is a plus if you're in a half-crazed state of mind from being lost. And unlike many recipes that require exotic ingredients, like pickled banana seeds or tiger's milk, these recipes include only ingredients that folks will recognize. The first recipe is a favorite of mine from my wife's grandmother and is on a list of my ten favorite foods: raspberry pancakes. The mix of sweetness, butter and tart berries is hard to describe, and if you're eating these pancakes while lost in the woods, you won't even care that you're lost.

Grandma's Raspberry Pancakes: Mix together 3 eggs with 1 cup flour, 1½ cups milk and ½ teaspoon salt (optional). You'll notice (assuming it is still daylight in the woods and you can see anything at all) the batter has a thinner consistency, much like a crepe. Over a good bed of cooking coals (not a bonfire), cover the bottom of your lightly greased fry pan with the mix and sprinkle evenly with raspberries. The pancakes needn't cook long—like an over-easy egg. I top the pancakes with butter and a light dusting of sugar; delicious. Raspberry pancakes are among our grandkids' favorite foods and they'll pick raspberries whenever they come to visit if they know pancakes will follow. Very convenient for me. But what if you're lost and you don't like raspberries?

Fifty-some years ago a person could walk into the Mecca Inn, which now quarters BIC Realty on the main street of Cook, and order a piece of blueberry pie made by owner Alice (Arnold) Gustafson. Her recipe transforms a blueberry pie as lights and a star bring life to a six-foot balsam tree. It's obvious that with blueberry pie as a survival food, you'd need to stumble across a trapper's shack or remote cabin with a working oven to cook it. And while the chance of that is low, there really isn't anything else to do while being lost, so accepting the challenge will take one's mind off the thought of spending the night in the woods alone and in the dark. Again, this pie recipe is easy to remember.

Alice's Blueberry Pie: For this mouth-watering treat, simply cook up a traditional blueberry pie filling by boiling berries, cornmeal, sugar and a little butter. After the filling cools, add 1 cup (about two front shirt pockets) of fresh blueberries along with a splash of lemon juice. Fold the mixture into a pre-baked pie crust and you're done. No top crust needed.

If you think that putting these dishes together in the woods is difficult, you're right, and maybe the notion is far-fetched, but don't hold it against me. I'm just the recipe guy. There is another survival food provided by our wilderness that is as good as raspberry pancakes and blueberry pie and all you really need to cook it is a stick, but good luck trying to collect the ingredients for venison shish kabobs, eh?

Hairy Boys

Listening to the radio a couple months ago, a DJ recalled how his basic training for military service was pure misery. After that, he was off to the jungles of Vietnam, where he was fortunate to have survived, to which he added, "I wouldn't trade the experience for anything." It's a comment typical of many vets and it may seem odd given the fact that if you were to offer the opportunity to donate a couple years of life to share in misery, pitched battle and a questionable chance of survival, most people would run the other way. But this conflict of reason is common in young people who overcome difficult hurdles, and it touches on the rites of passage to adulthood. And, for the sake of this story, as the rites of passage apply to men.

In his book Iron John: A Book About Men, author Robert Bly contends that cultures through the ages recognized the need to help boys into adulthood and to understand the complexities of being human, which includes both feminine and masculine influences. However, he also contends the cultivation of men has taken a back seat in recent years. One reason given is that it's difficult to talk about masculinity without appearing insensitive to the inequalities that have been a large part of womens' history. As a result, he reports a decades-old trend where only sensitive, polite and tamed men who can cry are rewarded by society, therein leading to a "softness" that is artificial, if not insincere. The author agrees that men indeed need to be sensitive, polite and able to cry, but he goes on to say that the only way they can do this honestly is through discovering their masculine side, which he describes as wild, or, put another way, "rough around the edges," as well as our civil, social and empathetic feminine side. Without such discovery, he argues, insecurity in men abounds.

A quote from the book: "Through hunting parties and in work men did together on farms and cottages and through local sports, older men (elders and spiritual leaders) spent much time with younger men and brought knowledge of male spirit and soul to them. Much of that chance or incidental mingling has ended.... and many boys experience only the companionship of other boys their age who, from the point of view of the old initiators (elders and spiritual leaders), know nothing at all."

For centuries, cultures of all kinds indoctrinated boys into adulthood by initiations that separated them symbolically from their parents (with an emphasis on mothers) and at the same time accepted them into the spiritual clanship of men. These rituals might include tests of strength, resolve, pain or responsibility, many of which would make most mothers wince. Most importantly, by the end of the ritual, boys were recognized publicly as having come of age and it was at this crossing that a boy grew into a well-rounded adult. As antiquated as this may sound, the author further argues boys and pain are synonymous. Cuts, bumps, bruises and breaks among boys are a common thread and the significance of the sacrifice of pain is something innate in all men. Football, wrestling and rough play are modern examples. He points to a mythical tale by the Grimm brothers from the early 1800s that tells of a large, hairy man laying at the bottom of a deep forest pool. The hairy man symbolizes the wild, instinctive side of man that all men must somehow encounter to be comfortable with their masculinity, and it takes courage and encouragement to go down into the pool. One reason men are singled out for this need of "fixing" is not that they need something special, but rather that women through the centuries have done their own version of bringing girls into adulthood, and they do it better. They find more places where young girls share opportunities of learning and bonding with elders beyond their mothers.

Famous actor-humorist Will Rodgers once said, "All I know is what I read in the papers." Likewise, I can't verify if all this is absolutely correct, but it offers reason and the author has done a lot of homework. When I was nine years old, my father shocked me when he asked if I would disk the fall plowing on our farm. He showed me how to operate the tractor and where to run the disk. I was so small I had to stand up to operate the clutch or the brakes. It was a giant leap from picking eggs or putting away my toys for my mother and it was a sense of responsibility that I'll never forget. Did my father really need help or did he just want me to grow up?

As soon as I finish this, I'm off to play basketball at the North Woods School with other basketball nuts. Upon returning home, I will surely be sore and bruised and just as surely, I will tell my wife, "It's a good hurt." Maybe it's a small version of "I wouldn't trade the experience for anything." And it's not such a stretch to think also that our Grizzly basketball team is an example of an initiation, just as a military experience may have been for our DJ friend. Our boys go off with elders (coaches) and learn important lessons in team building, sacrifice, pain, responsibility and integrity. And of course, the same could be said of girl teams as well. These kids, as Robert Bly would appreciate, may not be so much about wins and losses but rather discovering something deep inside about themselves, even spiritual things. Basketball has long been my passion, but maybe nowadays, I'm just going to the gym to greet that hairy man at the bottom of the pool again. It might be nothing more than that.

Good form, Grizzlies. Good form.

In the Year 2525

"In the Year 2525" was a popular song in 1969, sung by Zager and Evans, and it made haunting speculations on the state of mankind should we survive the centuries. And while it's only a song, the words inspire thought. I can't begin to imagine what the year 2525 will look like, given the seismic changes during my lifetime, which included the invention of microwave ovens, the hula hoop and Velcro, to name a few. Yup, after seeing Velcro I figured almost anything was possible. One thing you can count on is that the future will be shaped by what we do now. Consider world population.

The population of the planet is expected to increase by one billion people by the year 2030, to 8.6 billion. That's not far away and given that, it seems somebody should be preparing because there's a lot of work to do. To get your mind around just how big one billion is, here are some examples. Put a billion folks in a single-file line to buy opening-day Twins tickets and you'd have a line that stretches around the world eleven times. If each of these people someday wants to own just one 60-watt incandescent light bulb, we'll need to build fifty large (1,200 megawatt) power plants to drive them. We could cut this to five power plants if we used LED bulbs, but let's face it, folks like their cheap incandescent ones. We'll need 15 million dairy cows to provide one glass of milk every day for each person, and a real eye-opener: a stack of one billion pages of the Bible would stand forty-five miles high. For comparison, a jet plane that's little more than a speck as it flies over your house is six miles up.

So what can we do with information like this? Well, you can do what you want, but for my part, I will no longer complain about crowded lines to buy Twins tickets. And I won't curse loons or eagles for waking me up in the morning because it means we still have wilderness places. I'll buy LED light bulbs because they make sense and if Pearson's Rice River Dairy Farm near Cook sells stock shares, I'll buy that too.

Kidding aside, what is our world to do with another billion people? We've done it before, since world population was 3.6 billion in 1969 and has grown to 7.6 billion today, but it hasn't exactly been a picnic. I watch the news—quite a bit, actually—and there is a wealth of misery in the world.

The United Nations estimates 795 million people suffer from chronic undernourishment and 11 million of these are from developed countries. Throw in war, ethnic cleansing, systematic suppression of women, terror groups, homelessness and disease and you find a real mess… if you look.

We're fortunate to live where we live and to have what we have, but it will be increasingly difficult to enjoy our good fortune if increasing masses of people are starving. The world needs to do something. US farmers are more than capable of producing enough food. Sympathy is nice but inspired teachers teaching, skilled craftsmen building and caring doctors healing are better. After all, it's hard to get a job in Bangladesh if you can't read, you suffer from malaria and you spend your days digging roots for supper. And somehow, world leaders have to agree on a level of conduct that will not allow horrible behavior by groups or governments.

If you are looking for a list of near-impossible tasks, the notion of fixing the world would be at the top of it, but I have hope and the world has, if nothing else, lots of money. The world's richest man, Bill Gates, is a very generous man who is setting a great example of individuals who are sincerely trying to cure world ills with their fortunes. His $86 billion in worth (at this writing) when stacked in $100 bills would reach fifty-eight miles into the sky. That's a lot of money even in Cook, Minnesota, but it's peanuts compared to the trillions of "disposable" wealth in the world that we (you, me, Bill and some others) hold collectively. If trillions can finance war but can't provide cures, then I think we'd better start looking through that stack of Bible pages in search of more wisdom. Long story short, Bill leads the way but he needs our help. There are many ways you can help… if you look.

In the year 2525, if man is still alive, if woman can survive, they may find…

Santa-Navigating Technology

'Twas the night before Christmas at the two o'clock hour,
The household slept comfy while cell phones charged power.
Stockings were hung off our brand-new sound bar
On the table for Santa: GPS for his car.
When out in the yard, there arose such a clatter,
I sprang from my bed and quick emptied my bladder.
"The carpool is early! No time to brush teeth!"
My hair was a mess, like an old Christmas wreath.
Then I plugged in the coffee and unplugged the phone,
I searched for some clothing, then let out a groan,
'Cause it dawned on me cruelly—it's not a workday.
So, I went out to yell at my carpool friend Ray.
But Ray was not there, only me and the night.
And something was different, something not right.
The LED walk lights cast a shine on the snow,
Showing two narrow sleigh tracks dug deep in a row.
The sight quickly gave me a strange sense of dread.
If those tracks met the hot tub surely someone was dead.

Leo Wilenius

When what to my wondering eyes should appear,
But a round, bearded man dressed in red and some deer.
They were wandering around as if lost in space.
The guy dryly asked, "Where do you park at this place?
I thought that those yard lights would outline a landing,
But I'm telling you, man, I'm just glad to be standing.
There's a satellite dish and AC on the roof.
A security camera almost caught Prancer's hoof!
The tower next door bent up one of my skis.
I sure long for the days when I only feared trees!"
Then he gave me a wink and went straight to his work.
His wristwatch iPuter listing every small perk.
Then back to his sleigh he sat down on his throne,
As his jet-aided deer sleigh rose up like a drone.
"Now Dasher! Now Prancer! Now Comet and Cupid!
Just because we have rockets don't think that I'm stupid;
I installed a Fitbit and don't mean to be boasting,
But I know when you're pulling and I know when you're coasting.
On Dancer! On Blitzen! On Vixen and Donder!
Let's head off to Togo and thereabouts yonder.
To the Junction's front porch, to the Carpenter Hall,
Then dash on to Nelsons' and then to Dale Schall."
And I heard him exclaim as he rode out of sight,
"Good thing for technology or I'd be here all night!"
And he yelled out once more, and he said it with cheer,
"Merry Christmas to all and I'll see you next year!"

In the Beginning

The story of our existence is a good one with two competing theories: evolution and creation. The last thing I want to do is misrepresent the Bible, so let's look at the history of the universe and life on Earth in as much as science agrees. Of course, it's necessary to abbreviate, lest we take up the entire Cook News Herald, which is a preposterous idea since this paper can't exist without life-giving income from advertising any more than you and I can thrive without cell coverage. So let's get to it.

Fourteen billion years ago, there was nothing but a "singular," which was an ounce of matter squeezed into a speck so small, billions upon trillions of them would fit into the period at the end of this sentence. That is all there was—no space, no void around the singular, just this speck containing enormous energy. Then the singular exploded (Big Bang), creating our universe and reaching 100 billion light-years across in a matter of seconds. It's a lively time for heat and nuclear reactions, to say the least. Electromagnetism, gravity and elements came to be. We're fortunate gravity isn't too weak, otherwise the universe would be floating about forever without forming anything. On the other hand, if it was too strong, the singular could collapse back to a speck again and you know how frustrating that would be, especially if you just took a shower.

Einstein's theory of relativity proves our universe is a never-ending bending of sorts—you cannot reach the edge of the universe and there is no anything beyond the edge, even if you could get there. If you tried you'd probably end up where you are right now. I'll let you chew on that on your own, but if you take the time to check the math, it adds up.

We'll need to bypass a spectacular party of stars, quasars, galaxies and planets forming for the next 10 billion years, up until the time the earth cooled enough to become the only place in the known universe with conditions necessary to support life as we know it. Protein must be present to create life, so it was essential that over 1,000 amino acids linked together in a precise sequence that was so unlikely it makes the odds of getting hit by lightning daily for a lifetime a better bet. And where did amino acids come from? It's thought amino acids formed spontaneously and landed on Earth from a meteor.

Now we take another leap in time, when a tiny something like a cell with amino acids present took in nutrients and duplicated itself. This first pulse of life, this one "thing," to all you plants and animals reading this, was your first ancestor. After a couple billion years, cells specialized to plant or animal until lots of carbon and oxygen in the atmosphere provided for the creation of microbes, then little creatures of all sorts until a mudskipper-type animal crawled onto the beach 500 million years ago. This specimen was a crude prototype for humans, complete with two eyes, a nose, lungs and a mouth. Hair and a taste for barbecued venison would come only after millions of years of dinosaurs ruling the swamp first.

Maybe waiting this period out was the first sign of human intelligence, since I'd rather not deal with velociraptors either. (That's my idea, not science.)

And while the evidence of evolution is plentiful, some questions persist. How did birds, for example, come to be, since a lizard that eventually turns into an eagle would need to survive untold generations with partially formed wings, making them easy targets for extinction. Whatever the case, I'm just glad our mudskipper flourished and eventually gave rise to apes, our relatives that had split from an ancestor that was also common also to humans. Apes developed 25 million years before humans, but they still live in trees and can't spell. (Neither can I, but that is just a coincidence.) Indeed, we humans have done well, for if the entire 4,000,000,000 years of life on Earth were represented by a scale of one year, modern man's 200,000-year existence would cover only the last twenty-five minutes.

You may have noticed that even science takes a "leap of faith" every now and then in order to fill voids where evidence is lacking. After all, even a singular must have a mommy otherwise we assume the supernatural, since "existence" without a past makes no sense scientifically—the chicken or the egg question. I am a big fan of science, but I'm also a "believer." And if science can take a leap of faith when it needs to explain what cannot be explained, I find no conflict in having faith also in things that are mysterious in the body of evidence of an all-knowing and loving God. Both science and faith believe there was one single point of beginning—is that so surprising? I don't understand it all, perhaps nobody can, but these things don't oppose each other in my mind since faith, wisdom and knowledge are necessary to both versions of life. And rather than arguing over turf, together they tell one miraculous story of us.

A Nut on a Hill

Science is a complex subject, so it only stands to reason that teaching it must be difficult as well. It was my good fortune to have John Geiselman as teacher for physics and chemistry at Cook High back in the seventies, and he had an amazing ability of taking complex subject matter and paraphrasing it into terms even I could understand. Now, maybe you never thought about whether the chicken or the egg came first, and maybe you don't care whether infinity is or isn't (if you happen to know, give me a call). But those things don't affect us on a daily basis. However, the concept that energy can neither be created nor destroyed, only changed from one form to another, is a phenomenon happening all around us all the time and it's an intriguing scientific fact. So, with all due respect to his memory, let's look at ever-changing energy as Mr. Geiselman might have taught it, by the simple example of a nut on a hill.

To clarify, our little round nut is like the kind you eat, not like the neighbor you live next to. For this example, we'll include several types of energy: kinetic (energy of motion,) potential (energy of position), mechanical (energy applied to move an object), chemical energy (energy in BTUs), solar (energy of light) and thermal energy (heat). Our little nut is named Gary, and this is no reflection on the editor of the Cook News Herald or the owner of the Tire Shop.

And it goes like this: Sitting atop a hill one clear day, Gary (the nut) absorbs light energy and converts it to chemical energy in the form of the fruit inside his hard shell. Gary also represents potential energy due to gravity, which forever wants to pull him from his tree and to the bottom of the hill. Gary, by the way, has twice the potential energy than another nut (named Donny) who is perched halfway down the hill. Still with me?

As the day goes by, more thermal energy converted from solar energy grows on the surface of the earth, spawning air currents of kinetic energy called wind. When the wind collides with Gary, it gives up kinetic energy while changing to mechanical energy, which is the force that knocks Gary off his branch and down the hill. Once Gary begins rolling down the hill, he loses potential energy as he gains kinetic energy. As he collides with other objects down the hill, he continues to lose potential and kinetic energy while producing still more mechanical energy.

Finally, Gary the nut rolls to the bottom of the hill, where he bumps into a squirrel and settles to a stop. The squirrel (named Rocky) eats the nut for the delicious chemical energy contained in the fruit, which energizes him with the BTUs needed to carry on his day, producing heat and mechanical energy while gaining potential energy as he climbs the hill in search of other nuts, continuing on in a never-ending series of energy interactions. There you have it. Okay, I realize I'm no John Geiselman, but you get the idea.

I think an analogy can be made between energy and human beings: whatever you say and do affects and, indeed, infects other people in ways that carry on, just like energy, and this can be good or bad. During the Christmas season we should remember those who need our help and the many opportunities we all have to brighten the day for another. And beyond just remembering, I hope you'll be energized, like the nut rolling down the hill, to make positive effects on others. Be charitable. Reach out in a spirit of community to those with whom you don't always understand. It's Christmas time.

If you had Mr. Geiselman as a teacher, you may have noticed in the last paragraph we experienced another one of his traits by wandering away from the topic of science at the end of his class hour to share things that are important apart from science. He was a great guy and an exceptional teacher, and if this little story sheds light on his ways and the topic of ever-changing energy then maybe it was worth it, eh? If it didn't, blame the squirrel.

In Season

It seems odd to declare creamed cucumbers and onions as my favorite food but it is—right now. I'm eating the stuff as fast as my wife, who is one fantastic cook, by the way, will make it and yes, that was a not-so-subtle plea for more. We currently have cucumbers and onions coming out of our ears from a garden that rebounded from successive poundings of rain and hail earlier in the summer. There's something about fresh food from the garden that defies description and if you've never had fresh creamed cucumbers and onions, I doubt you'll understand. All I can say is that it's what's in season.

When I was growing up in rural Cook, it was apparent that folks had an affinity for the bounty provided by farm or field. Fall in the neighborhood was butchering time, providing fresh fried chicken, beef roast, pork chops and whatever small game I managed to shoot, to name a few. Fall was big in meat. I don't recall nature or the farm providing much of anything fresh during the winter, other than a few northern pike my father speared. But soon after the warmth of spring took hold in earnest, we could count on wild strawberries for shortcake, then blueberry pies, raspberry jam, rhubarb sauce and wild plums. Once the garden kicked in late in summer it showered us in all kinds of treats, including creamed cucumbers and onions. Eating what's in season makes sense for all kinds of reasons. For one, it answers the question, "What's for supper?" Furthermore, it's simply good manners to receive, with appreciation, a gift that is given. The forest, the field, the garden, the farm, the Lord or Great Spirit, depending on how you choose to think of it, are basically saying, "Here is this bounty. It is healthy and tasty and plentiful—right now. It is in season. Enjoy." Some will argue that the efficiency of small gardens or wild harvest is not relevant today given busy schedules and a large populace, but I'm enjoying fresh creamed cucumbers and onions that we picked from the ground thirty feet from my house. That's worth a lot to me—the worth just doesn't fill a wallet.

The best example of eating in season I know of was the

Ray Raati family, who lived in our neighborhood, and I was fortunate enough to experience their skills firsthand. When blueberries were ripe, the family would pick what I guess to be fifty gallons of them, then together they'd sit before a large fan as the whole family dutifully picked debris from the berries, which they laid out on a clean white sheet. Once a troublesome bear was turned into 150, maybe 200 pounds of ground, dark red meat, which was then heaped onto a large table, where aromatic spices were tossed on one by one by Ray. This was then mixed in by many hands, who in turn fed the meat into the sausage stuffer, where hundreds of hand-twisted sausages fell into large awaiting tubs. When wild rice was ripe or herring runs filled Lake Superior or apple orchards bent to the ground in Wisconsin, Ray and his wife, Louise, would collect large quantities of these meats and fruits to create savory dishes and reams of meat in their large smokehouse. Not only that, they'd generously bring back extra for other folks who might be wanting. Ray, a professional welder, had quite the reputation for producing works of art with wild foods, but truth is, it was Louise who, with the help of Ojibwe heritage, came to the marriage with most of the know-how. Whatever the case, it was always difficult for me to sit next to one of the Raati kids on the bus with my tuna sandwich and orange when one of them was packing freshly smoked herring or bear sausage. Many was the time I would have traded my treasured Daniel Boone lunch box for their goods.

Thinking about nature's gifts, I wish I could have experienced the buffalo, the once largest herd of animals in the world that thrived on the rich native grasses of our vast Midwest. What a sight that must have been, one that rivaled the spectacle of the Grand Canyon or the endless ocean blue. Then, in little more than one lifetime, the bison herd was culled from 60,000,000 animals to only 300, while at the same time, prairie grass was plowed under. It seems rather than accepting a seemingly limitless bounty (60 million buffalo is a lot of food any way you look at it), folks worked their hands to the bone to raise, house and protect domestic livestock while planting crops that withered in droughts or drowned in the wet. Maybe this and the fate of bison was as inevitable as the rising sun, and I'm not looking to either understand or blame generations of past. After all, buffalo do roam, as the song says, which would make anyone nervous if supper is grazing a couple states away. However, the song also suggests the buffalo was a desired part of a home on the range and that dream is essentially gone. It's sad. Who knows? Perhaps a delicacy in these parts two hundred years ago was buffalo steak and onions. The thought makes creamed cucumbers and onions look pale in comparison, but it's what I have now. It's what's in season and it's delicious.

Minnesota

An exhaustive study using thousands of points of data measuring things like education, health care, opportunity, economy, infrastructure, crime, fiscal stability and quality of life shows that Minnesota ranks among the top states in all the nation. The study conducted by the prestigious US News

& World Report shows that Midwest states in general are "ahead of the game," with three states in the top five. Minnesota's neighbor to the south, Iowa, rates #1. Minnesota ranks #2 and North Dakota, our neighbor to the west, rates #4. This information shouts out loudly that we are fortunate to be living where we do and I, for one, am not surprised by this discovery. But seriously, only #2?

To clarify, I've nothing against Iowa. After all, Iowa is a neighbor and every person I've met from Iowa has been likeable as long as they're not sitting on my secret fishing hole. Not only that, Iowa is first in corn production, which translates to lower-priced taco shells, and they're first in hog production, which translates to millions of pounds of bacon. Mmmm, bacon. When it comes to famous entertainers, Iowa is the birthplace of the likes of John Wayne, Buffalo Bill Cody and Michelle Bachmann, while Minnesota produced Judy Garland, Prince and Bob Dylan, and despite their having John Wayne, I think we have an edge.

And I know it's not polite to brag, but Minnesota has moose and mountain lions, timber and taconite, wild rice and Minnesota nice, microbrew ales and snowmobile trails and national parks—big fish but no sharks. Minnesota serves as headwaters to the largest body of fresh water in the world, Lake Superior, and to the Mississippi, the largest river in the US. It has over 11,000 lakes, more than one could possibly explore in a lifetime and on Lake Vermilion, there is an island on a lake on an island on a lake. Good grief, Charlie Brown (yes, he was "born" here too), we even have a state muffin: blueberry! Can Iowa say that? And I'm not done.

Guess which state in the union has the highest average ACT scores for high school seniors in the US? Yup—Minnesota. And with all that brain power, it's little wonder Minnesota features the Mayo Clinic, the top-rated hospital in the country and the Cook Area Hospital, which features a half-dozen dedicated doctors to serve us wood ticks at the end of the road in the northland. That sort of thing doesn't happen in a lot of states. Did you know there are more Fortune 500 companies per capita in Minnesota than any other state? Minnesota is home to Target, Best Buy, 3M, Hormel, Polaris and General Mills, to name just a few.

Oh, Iowa, why did you have to spoil our chance at number one? Many of you are Minnesota Viking fans, too, so surely you must know our frustration with finishing second place, even though that in itself is quite an honor. And while Minnesotans rejoice in achievement, our state fair, our beloved Minnesota Wild, Timberwolves, Gophers, our World Champion Twins and the Lynx basketball title machine, we still have to live alongside Wisconsin—a state, which, in 2010 (as we are reminded of all too often), was the champion cheese producer yet again.

Perhaps I digress, because this really is not about Iowa or Wisconsin. And who knows? Maybe Iowa edged us out for first place because they have better neighbors than we do. Think about that. All I know is that we were close and in true Minnesota fashion, I'll have to accept close as good enough. After all, a little humility is always a good thing. Hey! Maybe we'd be first in that too! Chances are more than good that the folks at US News & World Report didn't figure in just how great we are at humility. Good grief.

First Kiss

Maybe science wasn't "your bag," as we used to say, but if it wasn't, it may be that you didn't get the creative version of science as I did with my chemistry and physics teacher, John Geiselman. I've noted before that Mr. Geiselman could relate scientific principles into everyday life, such as how the laws of motion relate to a tackle in football or why a chemical reaction might be similar to a first kiss. With stuff like that, he not only had me listening, he had me taking notes, and I'm greatly interested in science still. Given this background, I thought it would be interesting to take an abbreviated look at electricity in the human body. It was either that or review my recipe for French toast. Such is the world of deadlines, eh?

When asked, "What makes you tick?" most folks answer "a loving spouse," "family" or "inspirational work," but it could also be "a motorcycle," "a trip to Vegas" or "deer season." Either way, I'd recommend you go with the spouse-family-work thing if you feel the need to go public. But the "tick" I'm referring to is of course the electrical system that makes everything you do possible. Electrical signals control your movement, sight, speech, hearing and thinking just as surely as a first kiss produces anxiety, but that's basic stuff you probably knew already.

Looking more closely, the body is made up of billions upon billions of atoms, each having either a positive or negative charge and each capable of instantly switching between positive and negative when called upon. So, instead of a switch turning on a linear circuit to power, let's say, a light in your home, your body is an intricate matrix of spontaneous communication between atoms in all directions under the guidance of your brain, which in our example can turn on every light on in the house at the same time or any variation therein. This very simple language of positives and negatives is in some ways like a computer system that can work on massive amounts of communication using the simple digits "1" and "0."

Most electrical activity is associated with signals to and from the brain, but another collection of cells in the heart, called the SA node, creates the rhythmic electrical impulses that makes your heart contract at a typical 72 beats per minute for your entire life, or 120 beats per minute at the sight of a big buck on opening day, or 200 beats per minute before a first kiss, which is just a guess on my part since that was a long time ago.

How much electricity do you have? Your body operates on about 10 to 100 millivolts, which is a small amount considering the battery in a smoke alarm is 9,000 millivolts. However, since the power needed for communication is infinitesimal when compared to performing mechanical work, it is sufficient. You can compare this fact to the tiny battery needed to power a cell phone versus the behemoth required to start your car.

You may want to keep in mind that you are an electrical system. Avoid lightning, for starters. For healthy operation, your body requires good hydration and a balance of foods that provide essential electrolytes such as sodium and potassium in order to function properly. Pizza happens to be an excellent source of sodium and potassium and it's a great meal for a first date, which of course could lead to a first kiss, but we simply don't have the space to cover gravitational forces here. If you find yourself in that situation, you'll just have to figure it out for yourself. Bring a calculator. Or not.

Ice Sharks

I'm not good at ice fishing but it doesn't stop me from trying. For one thing, it's easy—just drop in a line and wait for the next bite. And I've done it long enough to know hazards specific to ice fishing that folks should be aware of. You won't read about them in the Minnesota Department of Natural Resource's (DNR) fishing synopsis, so let's cover them here for newcomers to the sport. You can thank me later.

First is the notion of going alone. Fishing solo may sound cool, but it's not when you wait for a next bite that doesn't come. I promise that soaring eagles, foreboding cliffs and stately pines will not appease the numbing boredom that takes over when fishing is slow, which is not so uncommon with ice fishing. Thinking happy thoughts won't help, either—tried it—works for maybe five minutes. On the other hand, if you're really tired of the rat race and busyness of life, ice fishing by yourself is great therapy. After one day alone on the ice, you'll be eager to get back to making deadlines, working overtime and dodging rush hour traffic.

The flip side to ice fishing alone is going with others, which introduces yet another hazard. To be clear, sharing laughter, memories and snacks with friends and family is good stuff. But if you take away the gals, the young 'uns and rational people, you usually find yourself amongst friends or coworkers who convert, in effect, to "ice sharks," as I call them. It's a guy thing.

Unlike great whites, which explode from the deep to deliver one crushing blow, ice sharks loiter out in the open generally harassing their victims. It goes: "So, Joe, have you ever caught a fish?" or "This eelpout looks like your first-grade picture!" or "Shouldn't you call home, sweetheart? It's been fifteen minutes since you checked in."

Obviously, ice sharks don't talk sense, which may be why the DNR fails to mention them in their handout. Indeed, if you enjoy spirited discussion on the economy, healthy lifestyles or peace in the Middle East, this is not your peer group. But based on the DNR's position that most creatures big and small serve a purpose, ice sharks could someday become fodder themselves for even higher life forms within the ecosystem.

At least I hope so.

Hannah

It seems reasonable that the worlds of science and religion agree on many matters. One example, interestingly enough, is about the origin of man.

To start with, both disciplines recognize the fact that all of us, or almost all, are related—and that means you and me as well (a fact you may find distressing, but hopefully can reconcile). If you'd rather not accept that as truth, at the very least you'd have to concede that we're a lot alike. This is because all humans across the globe share about 99.9% of the same DNA. Only one tenth of one percent of your DNA creates differences in hair color, height, skin color, personality and facial features that add to your uniqueness.

Since unlocking the secrets of DNA, we can accurately track the migrations of peoples over the generations and across the globe. These studies show without a doubt that Asians, Europeans, Native Americans and Africans all share an origin in the continent of Africa. A person who looks Asian can have a greater proportion of European ancestors in their family tree than Asian ancestors and the same can be said on any other comparison you want to make.

In Bill Bryson's book A Short History of Nearly Everything, a point is made of the simple mathematics of our family trees. After twenty generations, you have over one million direct ancestors in the form of great-great-great… grandparents. Just five generations more and you have over thirty-three million ancestors and these of course are still just your grandparents, not to mention aunts, uncles and cousins.

It gets really interesting at the time of the Roman Empire, sixty-some generations ago, where the number of your direct ancestors is in the billions, which is more than the world population at that time. This math and DNA evidence proves that the vast number of people, in the sense of whether you think that you are Greek, Swedish, Kenyan or Japanese, are not "pure" lines. They can't be. Over the centuries, family lines and ethnicities crossed often. As the book states: "When someone boasts to you that he is descended from William the Conqueror or the Mayflower Pilgrims, you should answer, 'Me too!' In the most literal and fundamental sense we are all family."

My grandparents' names were Hannah, John, Alexsandra and Matt. Three of them passed before I was born and the other died when I was just five. It makes me envious of those who have had the gift of grandparents or great-grandparents in their lives. On the other hand, it's nice to know that Abe Lincoln, Sitting Bull and Dionne Warwick are part of the family!

The world would be a better place indeed if we could keep that in mind.

A Dose of Reality

Mr. Drysdale, a Beverly Hills banker, and his secretary, Ms. Jane, knocked on the door of the mansion where they were met by Jed Clampett, a Tennessee woodsman who had struck it rich in oil, and his daughter, Elly May. Proceeding to the billiards room, the group joined family members Jethro and Granny at the "fancy eating table" (the pool table) for a fine meal of baked possum, gopher gravy, grits and collard greens. Now that, folks, was "reality" TV at its best!

At least, it was as real as many of today's reality shows. The Bachelor is an example. The show brings together a group of perfectly capable women who do embarrassing public battle to win the heart of a man they do not know and who is conceited enough to allow such treatment of the woman he is assumed to eventually marry. Huh? This is the planet Earth, isn't it? If this is indeed the planet Earth and I'm not just having another weird dream, I need to ask the question: Which scenario (Jed or our latter-day Romeo) is more real? This kind of thing simply doesn't happen in the natural world, although I can't speak to algae and fungi.

On the other hand, there is professional wrestling. I know

a lot of people don't believe professional wrestling is real, but I do. What throws naysayers off is that wrestlers happen to share a close camaraderie in a competitive atmosphere. My wrestling heroes growing up were the Crusher, Dr. X, Cowboy Bill Watts, Vern Gagne, Pampero Firpo (the Wild Bull of the Pompas) and "Scrap Iron" Gadaski. And after having watched a wrestling match in person at the St. Louis County Fair, you can imagine my surprise when all these guys, who just minutes before were biting, kicking, choking, gouging and hitting each other with chairs, got into the same van at the edge of the stage (I assume to take them all to the hospital). What was really impressive was to see them laughing and congratulating each other as they were getting into the van. Now that is sportsmanship you just don't see anymore!

Backing up a bit, I do recall one episode of the Beverly Hillbillies in which Jed (who was an excellent marksman) shot a fly off the fence with his black powder rifle. It was my first experience of questioning reality TV. It's not that one can't shoot flies off a fence at 100 yards, but with a black powder rifle? It's unlikely at best, but since it was possible, I kept the faith. Hey, television is fun and I don't mean to rain on the parade of viewers of the Bachelor and shows like it because it's entertainment. But doesn't it strike anyone as odd that it's in the "reality" category instead of the "crazy idea that sells" category? Should we be so cavalier about lying? Reality should mean reality. Good grief, it's illegal for food companies to lie about what ingredients they put in a donut!

The truth must hold its nose quite often nowadays, but maybe it has always been that way. Tabloid magazines were around when I was growing up and a lot of folks enjoyed the doctored pictures and headlines they might proclaim, such as "Donny Osmond Marries a Blirkling from Venus—Expecting Kittens in June!" I'm sure Donny didn't appreciate that, but most folks got the joke and few fretted that he should have married an Earthling instead.

Love is a fickle thing, so maybe I shouldn't poke fun at shows like the Bachelor near the Valentine holiday. It will come as no surprise to anyone that a flock of girls never fought for my attention, but I was rather lucky to have a girl look my way twice. (I made the most of it!) Happy Valentines Day!

"Y'all come back now, ya hear?"

CHAPTER 2: YOUTH

The Learning Curve

Glorified Rice

I played a lot of one-on-none basketball on makeshift courts in our basement and kitchen at a very early age. I'd shoot baskets with tennis balls and ping pong balls in my room and I'd even dribble while in the bathroom. Ahem. Understandably, my identity (in my mind) was basketball, but the trait most recognized early in my youth was as a good eater. It's a talent that came naturally—my mom was a great cook and I was hungry. I like every potato or potato dish there is. Age six found me proficient at eating lutefisk, head cheese, salt herring, peas, blood sausage, fish head soup, corn relish, pickled pigs' feet, cows' tongue sandwiches and sauerkraut. Not so surprisingly, when I entered first grade at Alango School, eating was the least of my worries. But then, you know how that goes.

The school, or maybe it was my first-grade teacher and love of my life at the time, Mrs. Urich, had a policy that each student had to clean their plate at hot lunch because at that time, millions of children in China were starving to death. The logic made sense to me and the school year was going by just fine until the day I was introduced to "glorified rice"— perhaps the most deceptive name ever in the history of food.

Now, you might think I could eat anything, but that

wasn't quite true. There were just a few things that would not stay down and those were sweet pickles, Spam and raisins. To this day, if I am tricked into a sweet pickle at a graduation buffet, that pickle will come home in my pocket to be used as compost. It was lucky for me that the cooks at Alango, who by the way were great cooks, didn't like Spam and sweet pickles, either, but oh, did they like raisins, and they used them to make glorified rice. The ingredients in their glorified rice were simple enough: white rice, marshmallows, pineapple, cinnamon and raisins, but I will argue till the cows come home that these foods do not belong together in the same dish. Good grief, why not add ketchup, cornflakes and meat while you're cleaning out the kitchen, which is how glorified rice (in all likelihood) was discovered in the first place. Raisins, you may remember, are also famous for putting the "pop" in your fruitcake which, if we're going to be honest, is another culinary disaster by any measure.

For me, raisins are defined as perfectly good grapes that were left in the sun too long, then sold just prior to rotting. The Romans became big fans of raisins around 100 BC and the fact that Rome was a world power then, and is now just a city, speaks to the merits of raisins. But we're getting away from our story.

So, there I was, having finished a typically great meal such as green beans, mashed potatoes, and hamburger gravy, but with a spot of glorified rice still on my plate "speaking" to me. The glorified rice said, "Start gagging, pal. We ain't going anywhere." I didn't know what to do. I couldn't eat it, but I didn't want to disappoint my future wife, Mrs. Urich. But just as fate would have it, an angel of sorts appeared next to me in the form of classmate, Jimmy Beltramo. Jimmy had already finished his plate and why I remember this I do not know, but he started teasing me about my brown shirt. He nicknamed me "Brownie" and as we were talking there, the fact that he had finished his glorified rice got me thinking and as one might guess, I offered my glorified rice to Jimmy. But he didn't "bite."

As a kid growing up on a dead-end road, I didn't have a lot of experience in begging, but that day in the lunch room, I begged, pleaded and bargained with Jimmy Beltramo until he finally agreed to eat my glorified rice. Other than my pride, it only cost me an eraser or something like that. Then he easily gobbled down the rice in a few spoonfuls without gagging or even crossing his eyes—tough kid. In fact, he made it look so easy I wanted my eraser back, but a deal is a deal.

I don't recall encounters with glorified rice in the months to come, but I do recall the ability to fake illness in the first grade, one time stretching a couple days of chicken pox into a full week off. It surprises me still to think of that because I usually didn't want to miss school and disappoint Mrs. Urich, but coming full circle, there was probably glorified rice on the menu for that Friday. And just for the record, Mrs. Urich and I never did marry.

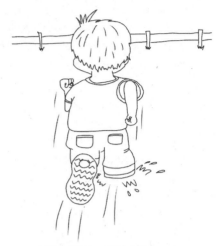

No Big Deal

The morning was overcast with a light mist filling the air, the ground saturated after an all-night rain. It was an unlikely setting for a day when two world records would fall in the field, which in this case was much like track and field, only it was a real field where cows lived.

We were standing out in Eino Ollikkala's pasture, located near the Greaney / Bois Forte line, where my dad and Mr. Ollikkala were surveying a large herd of cattle. We did that a lot, since my father was the agriculture and shop teacher at Cook High School. I wasn't fond of looking at cows, but my other choice for entertainment on a wet day of summer vacation was to wait at home on a dead-end road and hope that a baseball team would drop out of the sky. May as well look at cows.

You have to be a farmer to appreciate cow watching. To the untrained eye, they look the same, but in fact, they are unique, and farmers know most of them individually—probably because they watch them so often. Cows have a pecking order, which means boss cow gets the grain first. Some cows are tame, others crazy wild and those with horns know how to use them. Cows don't look athletic, but they can flat out fly and can jump tall fences if they have a notion to. Bulls get most of the attention because they are massive and yes, some will try to kill you if given the chance, but any kid who has ever had to play in a cow pasture knows that while bulls are aggressive, they are relatively slow. Country kids may be naïve in a city, but we're pretty wise to assessing dangers on the farm.

So, we're looking at cows and when you are eight years old, standing among them is like standing with elephants. Trying to stay with the men, I got too close to a cow that swung her head around, hitting me square in the chest and knocking me clean off my feet. Maybe it was an accident or maybe I was near her calf. Whatever the case, I was stunned but okay and apparently expendable since my dad and Mr. Ollikkala didn't make much of it. Having enough of this, I decided to wait back at our car, a brand-new, black 1963 Chevy Impala parked along the fence next to the road. Things got real interesting from then on.

Separating from the herd and heading for the car, I had the wherewithal to keep an eye on my back trail—yes, assessing danger. Soon, a bunch of curious cows that perhaps had never seen a small blond thing in their pasture before were looking my way, and next thing you know they were in stampede mode. Wanting to live another day, I peeled out of there like a cat with tons of "curious death" trailing right behind. The minefield of fresh cow pies had no effect on my straight-line trajectory to the car, as I set a new world record in the 200-yard pasture dash to the fence and then set another record in the forward lunge and roll diving under it. Huddled up next to the safety of the Chevy, the herd rolled up to a thunderous, bellowing, mud-churning halt just a few feet away. Getting rammed, avoiding a trampling and setting two records is a good day's work for a country boy. Curiously enough, it was no big deal since the men were still looking at cows. I could almost hear Mr. Ollikkala say to my dad, "You know, your boy there doesn't seem to care much for cows." And Dad might have responded, "Oh, he must like them some because we see him running with them at our place too. He likes baseball more though. Anyway, I'd keep a close watch on that cow on the right, Eino. Could be pink eye."

If it could be done, I'd like to go back in time to ask my dad or Mr. Ollikkala why so little fuss was made about me flying through the air from a cow contact or narrowly avoiding a trampling or setting two world records, but I can't. Apparently, people who grew up with the Great Depression, scarcity and world war had a high tolerance for things they needed to get excited about. That's understandable enough and I appreciate the calm that graces their generation. Perhaps a lesson from this experience was that the goal for the day was to watch cows, not entertain little Leo. Sometimes you just need to get with the program or get out of the way.

My dad loved me as much as a father could, and you know what? He didn't say a thing about his young son smeared in mud and cow dung sitting in his new car. It was no big deal. He made parenting look easy.

Pelican on My Mind

At least once a year I could look forward to our family pulling away from the dock at Cabin-O-Pines resort on Pelican Lake for a full day on the water. We brought fishing poles, of course, a can of angleworms, life vests, fishing hats and most importantly, a huge picnic lunch. It was so big it required a large cooler and a good-sized box to contain the egg salad, roast beef or tuna sandwiches on homemade bread, cinnamon rolls or cookies, fruit, a Thermos of coffee, a Thermos of milk and a jug of Mom's homemade lemonade. Not only that, my sister and I each got a bottle of Four-O or Bubble Up pop, along with a Mars candy bar or a Nut Goodie from the most magical resort store that ever existed (actually, all resort stores are magical), which was operated by the Mike Terska family.

The goal for the day was catching northern pike, because a good-sized pike was "it" for my father. A typical day of trolling also included a noon-time stop for a picnic lunch, some island exploring and a chance for my sister and I to catch world-class blue gills and sunfish from shore. "World class" is not just a boyhood imagination, and the fish statue in

Orr is there for good reason. If the world knew how big those fish were, Orr might look much different than the peaceful place it is today. Anyway, after a long day and with the sun waning in the summer sky, we'd troll back to the docks with a nice stringer of fish to a hero's welcome from Mike. It was good stuff.

One trip was most memorable for me. We were trolling spoons, pausing every so often to clean weeds from our lines. After clearing weeds during one these pauses, my mother reached back with both hands tightly clutching her fishing pole to cast her lure back into the water. She forgot I was sitting behind her and the treble hook on her lure now dangled an inch in front of my nose. With a mighty heave, she attempted to cast, but the lure caught the inside of my eyebrow as the drag of the reel and I screamed out in unison, to the horror of Mom.

Now you might think at a time like this, a six, maybe seven-year-old kid could really lay on the dramatics, but surprisingly enough I stayed calm—apparently eyebrows don't have many nerve endings. In a short while, Dad worked his magic with a pair of pliers, freeing me from the treble hook that had threatened to heave my young carcass starboard to the hungry pike. After taking a look at the damages and dusting me off, we threw our lines overboard and went right back to fishing. Yup, I took it like a man. That's the story the way I remember it—you know, just a little kid taking it like a man and all. I didn't call my sister to see if she had a different view of it, if she remembers it at all, since she was probably reading a book at the bow of the boat anyway. So that's it: impalement, horror, bravery, and modesty followed by a determined focus to continue fishing. I'm sticking with it.

Since that particular incident, I've spent many more hours chasing still more pike, along with crappies, bass and even walleyes on Pelican Lake. And the "iron eyebrow" experience would not be the last time I was impaled by a treble hook while fishing. But for some curious reason, I haven't returned to those small rocky islands to see if monster pan fish are still lurking close to shore, as they did so prolifically in my youth. Maybe the memory is so special I don't want to do anything to mess it up. All I know is that when the topic of fishing Pelican Lake comes up, I'm right back at the dock at Cabin-O-Pines with my plastic fishing pole waiting for another adventure. I don't know about you, but all this reminiscing has me itching to dig up some worms and hook up the boat. Hope your fishing goes well.

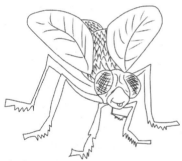

Horse and Flies

Bugs were a big part of my childhood. I'd watch them, play with them and experiment with them for hours a day. I'd rather have had a horse, but my parents said "No" with unwavering conviction so I didn't argue. However, a couple girls in our township, Sherry Rautiola and Roni Brunner, each had a horse, so I was fortunate enough to get a ride with them once in a while. I don't recall ever steering their horses, but I remember one time when Roni went full throttle with hers while I rode on back hanging on for dear life. Only those who have ridden as a passenger on a horse at full throttle can understand the terror I speak of. Clint Eastwood makes riding a horse look so easy, but then again, he wasn't riding behind Roni Brunner at full throttle. Anyway, no horse for me, so bugs it was.

I'd look for bugs in dirt, ponds, hayfields, dried cow pies, and under logs and rocks. Every so often I'd discover an exotic moth, beetle or a strange new species that would challenge me with questions such as, "Do I dare pick it up? Will it bite? Is it a bad bug? Will it taste good? Does this thing have a stinger?" I'm kidding, of course, about bugs tasting good—it's just one of those inside jokes we socially impaired bug lovers like to have fun with. I'll share what I've learned about bugs as a kid. To be clear, if you need specific information, say, for example, you're working towards a Master's degree in entomology, don't rely on this article as reference material. Call me.

Ants are fascinating bugs that mind their business, that is, if you don't mind them going about their business on your lawn, your sidewalk, at your picnic or in your house. I've dealt with many species, from big black ones to tiny blond ones, and while they are nice guys in the Minnesota bug world, I've dubbed them in the genus infestaceous indestructabus. In other words, get used to them because there's no way to get rid of them.

Wasps and bees are good bugs, also, but they have a bad rap given the "stinger" thing. I watched a wasp catch a horsefly once, which qualifies them for hero status in my book, while bees do the good work of pollinating and making honey. Wasps, it may surprise you to know, are also problem solvers. As a kid, a couple friends and I found a huge paper wasp nest across the creek at my aunt and uncle's farm. My reckless friends, with rocks in hand, stood under the nest pep-

pering it until a blinding mass of mad wasps made them retreat into the woods. I, on the other hand, would have none of
such foolishness, standing watch fifty yards away on a small
wooden bridge that spanned the creek. I was the only one
to get stung—not only that, but twice! It had to be that the
wasps saw little hope of changing the attitudes of my mur-
derous friends, so they figured, "Let's at least make sure the
blond kid over there never gets any funny ideas of his own."
I haven't.

Flies, that is, horseflies, deer flies and black biting flies,
are unnecessary, and that is the nicest thing I can say about
them. I know all creatures are supposed to serve a purpose
and that includes skunks, slugs, bloodsuckers, rats and even
our cat, Zippy. But flies? I don't think so. At our farm, hordes
of flies would run the cows unmercifully for part of the summer, sometimes driving them half crazy. It's well-known our
cows would run me about the farm, too, so it would be understandable if I were to consider this fair retribution. But flies
made my life miserable too. You just haven't felt the many
splendors of pain until you've been bitten on the back by a
horsefly, on the top of your head by a deer fly or on the ankle
by a black fly. I suspect mosquitoes are related to flies, but
they're slow and can be killed by the hundreds, which offers a
small satisfaction that makes summer campfires tolerable for
me, anyway. There's more I could say about bugs, but beetles
are boring and spiders give me the creeps. Enough said.

You know, winter gets long at this time of year, but at least
we aren't dealing with bugs, other than harmless snow fleas,
which really aren't fleas at all, but that's a fascinating story for
another day. Thinking of bugs makes me wonder how many
folks have paddled into the Boundary Waters for a wilderness
experience unaware and unprepared for them and came back
half crazed like our cows. I suppose that's why horseback rid-

ing is so popular—it lets you ride away from flies—but I can only guess about that since my parents wouldn't let me have a horse. If I could have had a horse, it probably would have been a quarter horse, but I would have gladly taken an Appaloosa, since they don't show dirt like solid-colored horses do. Actually, I would have taken any color or breed as long as it was about fifteen or sixteen hands high and as fast as Sherry or Roni's horse. A smaller, slower one would have worked though. Yup, a horse would have been nice, but I'm over it.

Home Remedies

As a boy, I watched my father level an old barn with his bulldozer when suddenly there was a burning sensation on my leg. Then another and another. It turns out, I was standing on top of an underground hornet nest that had been uncovered by the dozer and a swarm of them crawled up into my pant leg, doing their best to get me to move. "Move" is not the word for it, as I shot across the barnyard to the house screaming for help. After I arrived at the house, my mother quickly freed me of clothing in a frantic strip-down, but not before being stung many times. Now it was my mother's turn to do a mad dash across the barnyard, only she went to the pond, where she grabbed a handful of wet, cold mud and then returned to smear it on the stings. Next thing you know, I was feeling good. Dirty, but good. Now that's a home remedy I still swear by today, but we had others, some not as effective. Before the days of sunscreen, we just had sunburn, which was treated with (ugh) a warm bath. Now I'm not going to say that hot water actually had healing properties, but after the additional burn of the water, the sunburn actually didn't feel so bad. It may have been akin to hitting your toe with a hammer so you don't concentrate on the hurt from hitting your finger earlier. I wouldn't recommend it. We also drank 7 Up for upset stomach, treated a headache with a cold, wet towel on the forehead and unlike the old saying, "Starve a cold, feed a fever," we applied food to both as my mother couldn't find it in her heart to starve anything. All in all, these treatments worked well and Mom was not above referring to herself as "Dr. Wilenius" at times.

Other "cures" through my younger years were extremely effective. There was a time when I had some trouble controlling emotions. Some might call it temper tantrums. Whatever the case, after a few weeks of it, my mother discovered a glass of cold water liberally splashed on my head cured me in an instant. (Won't find that one in Child Rearing 101.) Several cases of Family Detachment Syndrome (threatening to run away from home) were treated with a fond farewell and best wishes for success in my new adventures. Boredom during the first half of summer vacation was treated with a 6:00 a.m. alarm clock leading to a day of cutting and peeling aspen trees in our back woods. Exhaustion, especially that resulting from the boredom treatment, was cured with ten hours of sleep. As a teen playing football, I had a bad habit of tackling high. During a football game in 1972, a fast, compact kid named Warner came around end and buried his helmet into my chest. That cured my habit of standing upright while tackling, but now I was on the ground wheezing with the breath knocked out of me. Unable to breathe, my well-meaning but dense teammates came up with the idea of picking me up by my belt and shaking me around a bit. That does not work. But from that experience I can tell you that it is possible to still be humiliated while you are in what seems to be last moments of life. To save you the suspense: I lived. And not only that, I still tackle low on the rare occasions that I actually catch up to one of my grandkids during a football game in the backyard.

I could go on and on and on with remedies and you probably know most of them anyway. Such as how the pain caused by someone's excessive complaining can be cured with a simple, "Okay, you do it." Or there's the time-tested cure to, "It hurts when I do this," which is, of course, "Well, then, don't do that."

There is one phenomenon that defies reason and that is the science of physical therapy. Knee operations and shoulder issues have brought me to the door of our local physical therapists on more than one occasion. They seem to be a very nice group of people in general and their results are nothing short of amazing, but in case you didn't know, physical therapists tend to rely on the creed, "No pain, no gain." There is more I could say about this, but suffice to say, it is an odd path to feeling great again. And given the soreness in my joints lately, I should probably make another appointment. But for now, I'll take a hot bath, then eat a bowl of ice cream while watching cartoons because it's probably what my mother, "Dr. Wilenius," would have suggested. Who am I to argue?

A System

It was early morning as brothers from a neighboring place, Dennis and Charlie, and I meandered through the woods searching for a herd of cattle. You wouldn't think finding twenty cows would be that difficult, but in eighty acres of wooded pasture, a 1,500-pound Holstein doesn't show up much better than a fifty-pound black lab. Looking for cows was a common routine during the summer pasture period and we did a pretty good job of it because we had a system.

Sometimes we'd find clues as to the herd's location by finding platters of fresh "sign." You knew fresh sign from old sign because it was still warm. I don't recall how we knew the sign was warm and I prefer to keep it that way, if you know what I mean. Anyway, we'd search in spread formation, keeping quiet until eventually someone would bark out, "I hear it," and we would all stop and listen. "It" was the bell on the lead cow, Honey. Soon enough, three boys persuaded a herd of Holsteins to head for the barn and the morning milking.

This work defined a fair part of my summers for several years as a boy. My aunt and uncle owned a small dairy farm and when my uncle took ill, keeping the farm operating fell largely onto to my Aunt Helen. I wanted to help. Ten cows to milk and another ten or so younger stock to care for may not seem a big deal, but it was. Once we got back to the barn with the cattle, my aunt would always remind us, "Don't let the cows get to Honey's stall." Honey cherished the first stall in line, so we made it a point to let her enter the barn first. If Daisy, Rosy, Brownie or one of the others made the foolish decision to go for it, Honey would declare war on the perpetrator, the barn and anything else she could kick. It was udder chaos (sorry—one only gets so many chances at these) with hooves, hides, equipment and some foul words flying about, but it only happened a couple times because we had a system.

Life at the Nordlund farm wasn't all work. After chores on a hot day we'd swim in Bloodsucker Bend, a ten-foot-wide spot on the mud-bottomed, rock-strewn, mosquito-infested, bloodsucker-filled Gilmore Creek located behind the barn. You couldn't pay someone to swim in that little pocket of water today because, well... I just know that nobody would. We'd ride horse too. The horse, Peanut, a boy-eating cross between a Shetland pony and grizzly bear, was boarded at the farm, but belonged to the Vainio kids who lived nearby. Fact is, that horse hated to be ridden and maybe it never had been ridden. To compensate for lack of cooperation by Peanut, we'd get the beast's attention with a handful of clover while another would sneak up and jump on its back. A good ride usually lasted about three seconds or fifty miles per hour, whichever came first. In total, we probably didn't ride Peanut even for a minute over the summer. Playing the rope game in the hay barn was another fun thing we came up with. The barn had a rope-and-pulley system left over from days when hay was put up loose, rather than baled. When the barn was almost empty, two of us would climb the ladder to the ceiling where the pulley was, grab the end of the rope and jump. The kid on the floor had the other end and would skid across the floor into a small pile of hay that was left. Charlie and Dennis together outweighed me by three times or more, which meant when I was pulled across the floor, my velocity at contact with the hay bales approached that of a three-second Peanut ride. It was often a painful game but the teamwork, you'd have to admit, made for a good system.

I know my aunt and uncle appreciated our help those summers, even though we probably wore out our welcome at times with our antics between milkings. It didn't occur to me until years later just how difficult their situation was. Money was tight and there were few programs at that time to help folks through. It was necessary to keep the farm going as long as they could. Other family members, friends and neighbors helped, as well, until new dairy requirements and old farm equipment took their toll and the stock had to be sold.

But for several years, two boys, Dennis and Charlie, a couple of neighbor kids hardly in their teens, walked a half mile to help with chores on the farm every morning and they were there again, every night, to do the same. It seemed like fun and games at the time, but it was important for my aunt and uncle. I'm glad I could be a part of it. With angry hate groups in the news today promoting exclusion and looking for attention, it's good to remember there are many more folks out there volunteering, working with charities and helping their neighbors without looking for anything at all in return—just like Dennis and Charlie did. They were the system.

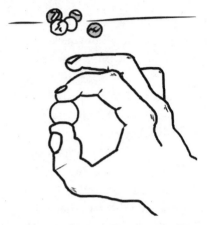

I Lost My Marbles at Alango

My grade school years at Alango Elementary were special for more reasons than I can recite, but near the top of the list was the annual spring marble phenomenon. I call it a phenomenon because it was predictable without any organized plan. Just as surely as mysterious impulses cause mayflies to hatch from the depths and snowbirds to return from Florida, nearly every student in the school would begin playing marbles during the noon break for a week or two each spring.

The games were simple. In "Cat and Mouse," you tried to hit your opponents' marble before being hit. There was "Circle," where you sought to knock your opponents' marbles out of a circle drawn on the sidewalk, similar to billiards. The most popular game had no name, and it was to see who could land their marble into a designated crack in the sidewalk with the least number of tries. And the stakes were high, because the loser in any one of those games lost his marbles as well.

I was a fair marble player with a collection of puries, cat eyes, steelies, butterflies and biggies (boulders), and it didn't take a rocket scientist to check out the competition since most kids kept their marbles in a pouch. A full pouch of marbles was a pretty good indication you were dealing with a serious contender. And as a credit to the social graces of Alango kids, each player meandered about from person to person, girls and boys alike, to challenge or be challenged on the marble battlefields. I don't recall much else about the phenomenon other than one particular day when I was involved in the Alango version of the shootout at the OK Corral.

Things had been going my way this particular season and my collection of marbles was considerable. But there was another kid on the playground who had amassed a collection bigger than most and I knew it was just a matter of time before we'd have to give it a go. Eventually and without fanfare, the day came when I finally met up with Jimmy Beltramo, the "shark of the sidewalk," for what was, in my mind, much more than a game of marbles. This was the same Jimmy Beltramo who just a few years prior saved me in the Alango lunchroom from a heaping helping of glorified rice, which is a poor substitute for real food and has no business in lunchrooms where young children are present. And while I appreciated Jimmy's heroics on that front, he was now my nemesis and he portrayed a confidence only a kid who had mastered glorified rice could muster. We had to play. It had to be decided. It was a point of honor. He beat me pretty bad. That's all I remember.

I can't say there was a lesson to be learned, other than marbles at Alango was fun—we'd lose a few, win a few and we did it without adult supervision. It was as good as it gets and it's a memory that comes to mind each year when the snows finally melt. Last spring while doing a highway clean-up with our grandkids, I mentioned to my grandson Alex that when I was a kid, we'd pick cans from the ditch then see how many we could keep going as we kicked them down the highway. Alex replied matter-of-factly, "I suppose you had to come up

with something since you didn't have an Xbox to play with."
He was probably right. Kicking cans and shooting marbles
might not sound very flashy or as fun as an Xbox video game,
but I think kids today are missing out on a pretty cool experience. For one thing, you needed other kids to play along, so
you learned important lessons in cooperation. And if by some
stroke of luck I should live to be a hundred years old, I'll still
have my marbles. On second thought, maybe it's time to give
those marbles to some other kid, because it doesn't seem right
to keep that much fun stored on a shelf.

A Long-Distance Affair

The spring track and field season was a big deal during
my high school days, with Cook and Orr providing powerful
teams year after year. You may not guess it now, but guys
with names like Glowaski, Leinonen, Brodeen and Crain
would sail over hurdles, toss large pieces of steel and run like
the wind. Apparently, I could, too, because I had a lead. A big
lead!

The pack of twenty runners trailed well behind, which
was not only exhilarating but hard to comprehend, since I
was a freshman in my first track meet. As we came around

the corner, our coach was waiting along the track, where he frantically yelled out those unforgettable words: "Slow down, Wilenius!" Huh? What kind of advice is that? I thought, but there was no time for questions. I just kept running like the wind. But before we go on, we need to go back to explain a few things.

Earlier in the day, our track team was on a bus to Babbitt for the meet when our coach, Floyd "Govie" Olson, stood up front to announce, "I'm looking for volunteers." He went on to explain that he didn't have any long-distance runners signed up for the two-mile event and very much wanted that condition to change. The silence was uncomfortable until three of us volunteered. It seemed like the thing to do for the team's sake—you know, "all for one and one for all" stuff. I should have kept my mouth shut.

In case you don't know, there is a strategy in the two-mile event where "pace" is extremely important. Sometimes you start out easy and sprint at the end, sometimes you vary the pace to disrupt the competition and sometimes you set an even pace to carry throughout. I knew none of these things because the quarter-mile race I had trained for is a sprint: green light, go fast, red light. It's pretty basic stuff not requiring strategy or pace. Now, back to the race.

"Slow down! Relax!" Coach yelled out again as I steamed into the next turn and into the back stretch of the second lap. It seemed my "go fast" philosophy was working since I was still ahead, however, the advice started to sink in as my energy began to wane and my muscles screamed for rest. As soon as we completed the second lap and headed into the turn again, someone behind barked out, "Let's go!" and a group of seasoned runners passed me with ease. The moment also marked the point where my body decided it had enough of this long-distance affair. The job at hand was crystal clear now, and that was not to win, but rather survive six more times around the track, which was as appealing as running to Wisconsin. After a few more laps, the group that passed me earlier passed by again. That is referred to as being "lapped," which in the track business is akin to being struck out, thrown for a loss, KO'd, pinned, blown out, swept, beaten and pulverized. I finished the race mentally and physically spent, but I finished.

If there was anything positive about the day, it's that a few other guys finished behind me. One of them was another volunteer, Al Baumgartner, one of the best pole vaulters to ever come out of Cook High School. Apparently, pole vaulters have little appreciation for pace either.

Despite the agony of this spirit-crushing, gut-wrenching, self-worth-robbing setback, I didn't give up on track. The pride of setting personal bests, the thrill of a win and the fun of just hanging in the infield on a spring day with friends kept me motivated—to throw the shot put. You'd be surprised how far you can throw a shot put to avoid running the two-mile!

Hunting: the Early Years

A brisk wind stirred in the trees as I carefully closed the truck door. It was a soggy morning before sunrise and I knew the walk to my deer stand on this opening day would be masked by the elements. The stand overlooked a forested deer trail connecting a feeding area with a swampy thicket. In a short time, as if on cue, a buck materialized on the trail, coming directly toward me on his way to the shelter of the thicket. It was so close, I had to slowly rise to my feet as it passed by in order to shoot over the side of the stand, where the buck fell in its tracks. This hunt just a few years ago was successful because preparations, elements and some very lucky timing came together that morning, but it's certainly not always that way.

When I started deer hunting as a twelve-year-old, I did so on my own because my father had no interest in hunting or the shooting sports. How to shoot, how to hunt and where to hunt, for me, were things learned by trial and error. If you haven't experienced trial and error before, consider yourself fortunate, because it's often painful and expensive. But my mother, always the cheerleader, encouraged me by saying I had "sisu" when it came to hunting, which is a Finnish word that, near as I can figure, must mean "Determined beyond reason. Willing to invest substantial energy and resources in elongated periods of disappointment and general discomfort for uncertain reward. Slow learner."

Before I could deer hunt, though, I needed a gun. After saving money earned by throwing hay bales and peeling aspen trees (it used to be a thing before machines learned how to peel bark), I talked my folks into allowing me to buy a new Winchester Model 94 .30-30, a lever-action rifle, from the Sears catalog. The gun finally arrived and as I opened the box, never had such a wondrous thing beset my eyes. Holding it for the first time, the solid feel and balance left little wonder as to why it was one of the most popular guns of all time. The smell of oil that glistened along the barrel. The feng shui of wood and metal—function and artistry. I had bought into a symphony of emotions that were well beyond my twelve years, but even a novice like me knew the gun needed to be sighted in.

Sighting in was easy. After a shot or two at a box set out in the pasture a short distance away, I found the gun was hitting about a foot to the left and a foot high—I simply needed to compensate by shooting low and to the right. (Remember, I was twelve.) Well, "compensating" might work in playing golf, but it happens to be a terrible way to sight in a gun. Still, when you don't know, you simply don't know. As luck would have it, that season a deer ran along a fence row in front of me and I dropped it with a shot to the "boiler room.". Then, a year later, I missed a buck standing broadside at a hundred yards, missed it again running toward me at seventy-five yards, then missed yet again as it ran in front of me at thirty. This was probably when I began to take reading seriously and soon thereafter learned how to sight in the correct way.

The early years I mostly "still hunted," silently coursing through the woods taking cautious and quiet steps, while stopping for minutes at a time to study my surroundings, hoping to spot a deer before it spotted me. But the phenomenon of building deer stands in trees was growing, and always one interested in new technology that doesn't include passwords, I figured I'd take a crack at it. My first deer stand was based upon two small spruce trees growing close together along the edge of a swamp. Years before, another hunter had nailed a few one-by-sixes across the two trees to a height of about six feet, where a narrow platform provided a spot to stand. Not satisfied with the height, I used the old stand as a ladder to access a new one I cobbled together above it with a pocket full of nails and rungs hued from nearby trees. It was as crude as the stand below it, but as established from the start, I was determined and a slow learner, and I would stand in my stand for hours until I eventually harvested a deer.

One year, I thought it would be fun to bring my girlfriend hunting with me and we would use the old "swamp stand," as it seemed to be made for such an outing. On opening morning, we walked a half mile to the stand through the frigid darkness in our fashion-correct, tight blue jeans and something red for safety. My instructions to her were simple. She was to sit on the first level (feet dangling) in an observational role while I would climb to the penthouse level to show off my hunting prowess and food-gathering capabilities. "And whatever you do, don't move and don't make a peep," I instructed. It was a couple hours into the still morning and as the sun cleared the horizon I noticed tree branches around me shaking. I looked down to see "the girlfriend" shivering uncontrollably as she sat there on a board in her jeans, her feet numb from the loss of circulation while dangling. Well, I thought I had made it clear that there was to be no moving, but truth be told, I was pretty cold in my jeans, too, so I came down to suggest that maybe we hunted enough for one day.

Eventually, I learned through more trial and error that dinner and a movie was a better way to make an impression than taking her deer hunting. A few years later we got married and I find myself still learning by trial and error in that endeavor, but that's another story. She never did take up deer hunting. Not enough sisu, I guess.

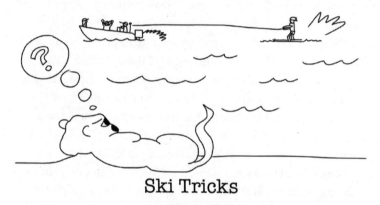

Ski Tricks

Have you ever arrived at a party late? It's awkward when everyone else is comfortable and having a good time while you stand there with your hands in your pockets just wanting to fit in. That's how I felt standing on the dock waiting to go waterskiing.

I love being in, on and around the water, so learning to waterski as a teen was a high priority, especially since there wasn't an equivalent video game. I learned to ski in the Oak Narrows area of Lake Vermilion. It was easy enough. Slap on two skis and let the eighteen-horsepower Evinrude groan for fifty yards or so as it slowly pulled you up and out of the water. Within a short time, you had the hang of it and could even show off at a not-so-breathtaking fifteen miles per hour. In fact, the pace was so slow, bringing a sandwich to munch on while waiting for the Evinrude to get you back to the dock after two circles around the bay seemed reasonable. That was waterskiing to me.

So, it was summer vacation after my junior year of high school and I got the call to go skiing with the guys. I don't recall if I packed sandwiches but the next thing you know, we (Steve Hill, Guy Pohto, Leon Long, Al Musech and I) were gathered on the dock at Musech's lot on Lake Vermilion. Looking around, the "late to the party" feeling engulfed me because everyone was pumped to get going while everything felt foreign to me. The eighteen-horsepower Evinrude was replaced by a motor much larger, the calm, confined waters of Oak Narrows were replaced by imposing Wakemup Bay and most notably, one of the skis was missing and replaced by nothing at all. Apparently, this was normal to all in attendance but me, a fellow who relied heavily on two skis to stay above the water.

As things got underway, I let the others go first while try-ing to think of an excuse to go home. They were all very good. One by one, each yelled for the boat to "hit it" while timing an explosive jump off the dock or from shore when the rope went taut, then cutting hard into the first of many graceful turns and water-skipping maneuvers. It was enough to make an otter jealous. To top it off, they didn't even bother to get wet, unless of course one decided to show off with a triple axle with a forward tuck and roll as he completed his run at the dock. It was obvious now that prior summers spent shoot-ing baskets and castrating bull calves had not prepared me for the initiation into this group of skiing maniacs. Out of time and excuses, but willing to suffer the consequences, it was my turn to strap on the ski.

It's really not important to report what happened after that, since catastrophic events are so commonplace in the news nowadays. But the day made me think about a scene in the 1990 hit movie Dances with Wolves in which the main character, Lieutenant Dunbar, played by Kevin Costner, playfully stumbles around in the prairie while chasing a semi-friendly wolf. This clumsy game of cat and mouse was witnessed by warriors of the local Sioux nation, who would later befriend the officer and give him a name of their own. From what they witnessed, it would have been accurate to name him Runs like Wounded Woodchuck, but instead they anointed him with the inspirational name of Dances with Wolves.

The guys that day could have given me a name or nickname, as well, that would have rightfully harassed me into the sunset. Instead, they worked hard to teach me to slalom ski, which I eventually did—more or less. And just like the natives were merciful with Lieutenant Dunbar, the guys were merciful with me—more or less. It may sound strange, but in a pack of guys, it is much easier to take harassment than accept sympathy, kindness and good intentions. I'm suspicious that their unusual hospitality was probably some sort of fiendish "kill him with kindness" trick that they laugh about still when I'm not around. Anyway, had they been smart enough to give me a name it could have been something like Blind Bear Drowning or Broken Muskrat Will Die, but since they didn't, I'll take the initiative for the sake of posterity and do it myself.

So, in the spirit of Chief Wakemup of the Ojibwe Nation, who I believe would have also been respectful in providing a name had he seen me skiing that day, I choose the name Swims with Otters. I don't know if that follows Ojibwe tradition or not, but it allows me a little dignity and even compliments the pack of rats that I used to ski with.

CHAPTER 3: PEOPLE

Good People for Good Reasons

Mrs. Davis

Often as not I couldn't tell you what I did a couple days ago, but the other night, while unsuccessfully trying to get back to sleep, I recounted the names of each of my teachers from first grade through high school. Not only that, I remember them as individuals, not just for the lessons they taught— how each handled his or herself, their sense of fairness and their commitment. Then I thought about Mrs. Francis Davis, my high school English teacher. She was extraordinary.

Mrs. Davis epitomized the ideals of "professional," which served her well in the unenviable task of teaching an expanded vocabulary to kids who, for the most part, cared little about the word "modicum." (Mo·di·cum—noun…mall portion, a limited quantity. / Leo's column in the Cook News Herald provides just a modicum of the income he needs to buy a motorcycle.) Daily, she would drill us in the spelling, definition and pronunciation of words, some of which we had never seen before and most of which we considered unimportant to our success in life.

Beyond professional, Mrs. Davis exuded confidence and poise. A gaze from her intense brown eyes told students who were not behaving everything they needed to "hear." In a meeting of kings and queens, popes and generals, chiefs and chiefs of staff, Mrs. Davis would have proved most comfortable. And she didn't relax when she was with our class. Pacing deliberately up and down the aisles in high heels and formal dress, she'd pronounce a new word in a clear and animated delivery that invoked every muscle of her lips, jaw and tongue to the fullest. In a staccato of syllables she would affirm, "The word is 'nu-CLE-ar,' not 'nu-CU-lar'" while intensely surveying the room for anyone who might differ and of course, nobody did. Watching her sound out the word "manipulate" was worth the price of a front-row seat. Go ahead and try it yourself, but to get the full effect, be very very animated: ma-nip-u-late.

Beyond her literary skills, Mrs. Davis wrote the book on posture. Whether standing or sitting, her posture was a pose that made the statement, "I am here. I am unflappable and I will be respected." Indeed, her posture would have served well as a training model for the Marine Corps. It's just a guess on my part, but if Mrs. Davis were walking down a hallway in a mall, persons belonging to any branch of the military would have felt the urge to salute.

It was fortunate for her students that Mrs. Davis kept her talents in the teaching profession, because she would have had a plethora of options. An example of her effectiveness, I happen to be a person who prefers the casual, spontaneous, simple and approximate in my approach to life, but she taught me to respect the need also for the formal, scheduled, complex and precise. (That was a curveball I didn't see coming in a high school English class.) Given the superlatives used to describe her, it would be easy but erroneous to think of Mrs. Davis as arrogant. To the contrary, she was approachable, fair, quick to help and sincerely welcomed an honest question. And last but not least, every so often a smile broke through her professional veneer that let us know she cared and enjoyed what she was doing.

When Mrs. Davis taught us the word "modicum," I doubted there would ever be a place to use it in conversation or writing without being run out of town. But now that I have, perhaps it qualifies as keeping the faith in her honor. Mark Twain once said that the difference between the correct word and the almost correct word is like the difference between lightning and a lightning bug. Mrs. Davis once taught that principle to kids who in time came to appreciate it more than she could know. On second thought, she probably knew that too.

My Sibling

Never was a thumb-sucker. And I don't recall having a "blanky" or a "Nuk" either. When you grow up on a farm on a dead-end road, apparently you don't need them. Actually, now that I think of it, one needs to grow up rather fast if for no other reason than you had to be fast to catch a Rhode Island Red or run from a Hereford, lest you be bored or trampled to death. But I did have (and still have) a sister— "Sis" or Leone to most folks. And for the sake of full disclosure, I was "Bruzz," Mom and Dad were "Mom" and "Dad," our cat was "Kitty," our beagle was "Poochie" and every week we would go to "town" for shopping. Yes, we kept it simple on the farm, but you have to admit, the system had clarity.

Having a sister for an only sibling isn't as tough as most people might think. We played together a lot when we were little. My mom said that Sis would stuff me into her baby doll carriage and parade me around the yard as an infant. When I got old enough, I'd catch chickens while wearing nothing but underpants (as documented by family photo albums) and then put the chickens in the baby carriage for her to push about in my stead. For the record, the underwear was accepted practice in dead-end road lifestyles for little boys at that time. Beyond that, we'd skate on the pond, make snowmen, explore and play with dolls, which was her idea and since I had nothing else going, I didn't argue about it.

Eventually, I became interested in bugs, sports and the outdoors while she degenerated into a life of dedicated school studies, socializing with people her age, band, listening to music and preparing for a career. It was a pretty natural separation. Playing on my own wasn't so tough. I spent a lot of time punting a football and running to catch it. I threw baseballs with the same theory and dribbled basketballs a lot. Eventually, a three-speed bicycle opened up a whole new world that included swimming, fishing and visiting friends around Sturgeon Township.

Before you know it, my sister was in college, then married to the "the boyfriend" and off to a military life making a home in many different parts of the country while I began to appreciate high school life and even girls. One girl was so distracting, I hardly noticed that Sis was gone. But come the holidays, there was an empty place at the table that just didn't seem right. I guess I was lonesome.

Growing up at the end of a dead-end road is unique in that not much happens there as compared to a lot of other places. Perhaps it's that scarcity that helps a person to notice things—little things, odd things and indeed important things. I got to know our neighbors, who were all quite elderly, even Mr. and Mrs. Vainio, who were in their nineties and spoke mostly Finnish. (I think they liked me.) I learned to appreciate quiet time and time alone. I learned to get along with kids because I didn't get that many chances at it. Last but not least, I appreciated my family, even my sister who was my playmate and best friend for years. For a long time I wanted a horse and a brother, too, but having a sister as an only sibling really isn't all that tough. It's pretty nice, actually.

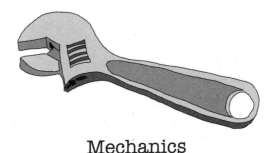

Mechanics

My father taught industrial arts at Cook High School for twenty-some years and to me he was a mechanical genius, just like his brothers or some of my cousins. There was nothing he couldn't fix, build or improvise. A statement I've made more than once is that if my father and Ray Hill of Hill Wood Products (another mechanical genius) would have had engineering training, together they could have landed a man on the moon ten years earlier than NASA and gotten there with an internal combustion engine—maybe a 454 Chevy big block. I suspect their spaceship would have looked cobbled together though. Think of an old fire tower frame, a repurposed water tank from a fire truck, the 454, some belts, a big recoil, pulleys, maybe some wings or propellers and "USA" spray-painted on the tank (they were mechanical, not artsy).

Despite the passing of my father and Ray, we are surrounded still by a good number of mechanical geniuses, since that seems to be the criteria of a good mechanic, which should come as no surprise to anyone. A car, for example, is made up of thousands of parts. To understand how these parts support, react to and work with each other nowadays takes knowledge in electronics, friction, hydraulics, electricity, chemistry, computers, the combustion process and more. To understand how these parts all fit together takes… well, I don't know exactly what that takes. Anyway, when you drop your car off at the shop with the astute observation that, "The motor is acting funny," your mechanic has to use all of the aforementioned disciplines, along with your helpful assessment, of course, to localize the problem in order to solve it. And you thought fishing guides were under pressure?

Fact is, while you're giving your assessment, your mechanic has politely moved on to contemplating the problem rather than entertaining your anxiety. Mechanics, if I may, are the gunslingers of the "Automotive West," more so than the race car drivers who tend to get most of the attention. Cool, calculating and focused, they efficiently get the job done and learned long ago that using a bigger hammer will not fix the problem. Usually, anyway. They know how to contort their body in order to reach parts on your vehicle that are unreachable. They use expensive computers to analyze an engine and if that doesn't work, they use a broom handle as a stethoscope to do the same and they make other customized tools to get the job done because these tools don't exist anywhere else. They know when it is metric and when it is not and they know what can be fixed or what should be replaced.

When I was a teen helping make hay on the farm, I was the operator and my father was the mechanic—a typical brawn and brains relationship, with Dad as the brains of course. I'd cut hay until a part broke on the mower, then while Dad fixed that, I'd take another tractor to rake hay on another field until something broke there, and so it often went. I tend to blame that scenario on the fact that we had very old equipment, but no doubt, many of our problems were due to my operating the equipment too hard and too fast. Now that I am the mechanic by default and must fix what breaks (excuse me for any inference that I'm a mechanic), I am more careful, I grease things more often, tighten things that are loose and generally baby our old stuff right through hay season with remarkably few mechanical issues.

If I could start over again, I wouldn't choose to be a mechanic even though my family pedigree is full of mechanical people. My skill set relates more to basketballs, fishing poles, coaching and hunting than it does to mechanical things, and I don't have the patience and focus of my father and folks like him. But I appreciate my father's skills and I continue to make hay and fix the farm equipment in his absence just to prove I can do it. I think he'd be proud, or if nothing else, very, very surprised to know the equipment still works. If only I would have taken the time to learn more from him. But that happens often enough, I guess. We don't realize just how much we have until he's gone.

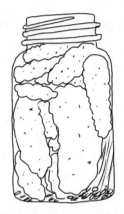

Irene's Pickles

Dedicated to our very special Auntie Irene
'Twas just another April morning
when someone gave a passing warning,

"Irene will have a birthday next.
What should we do? We are perplexed."

The answer was, "Don't have a clue.
Let's ask her daughter what she'll do."

But Gail said, "Don't think I'm rude,
'cause I took care of gifts and food.

We'll have some cake that's served in cups,
Mom's pickles and a ham from Zup's.

A program and that silly stuff
just ain't my bag. I've done enough!"

So, there we sat at half past nine,
with little ready and lesser time.

When came a groan, "Oh, what's the use,"
I knew 'twas time for Dr. Seuss.

So, hang on, folks, you'll feel the flow

of Dr. Seuss bip-bop-bing-low.

A man sat at the Country Store
upon the bench next to the door,

So, thinking he could use a friend,
I shared the bench—the other end.

And then to get him to say more
I shook his hand, spit on the floor.

And said, "Would you like a pickle, sir?
These are the best, you will concur.

They are as good as they can be
—might start some talk 'twixt you and me."

He quipped, "Why on earth would I do such?
Your request, my man—a little much.

I have no need to eat such things.
So please, let's talk of other things."

So, then I said, "What if you knew,
this pickle's from a secret brew?

And something else that will amaze,
made by the queen of Timber Days

Whose grandkids say she is the bestest
and that her heart is big as Texas.

Great-grandkids also sup on these!
So, take one, taste one, try one, please!"

"Oh no, I won't!" the stranger said
about the food he seemed to dread.

"Not a whiff will reach my snout,
so leave me now, go on, get out."

"But sir," I said, "Just have one bite.
I promise, it is pure delight.

She Won't Mow the Daisies

And if you don't enjoy it all,
I'll leave you quick, I will not stall,

But you should know this food ain't junk.
Ask Gary, Gail or even Punk.

And if one's feeling kinda fickle,
all it takes is Grandma's pickle."

He growled, "Why don't you seem to understand
my simple, sincere 'NO' command?

'Cause pickles never met me well,
they make my little tummy swell.

And if you don't leave on the double,
that pickle is your least of trouble."

So, with these words, I came to see
he feared the pickle more than me,

Then I replied, "Okay, I'll go,
but it's too bad you'll never know

The goodness that Irene has made
—this piece of heaven dressed in jade."

He yelled, "Hold on! You must be kidding!
And yes, I will oblige your bidding.

You didn't say Irene made these!
Forgive me, may I have one, please?

I've heard her goodness far and wide
and listen, I won't kid you, Clyde,

That goodness is too often wasted.
Sometimes you see it, sometimes it's tasted,

And those who've never had the feel
of something good and something real

Are often left to wonder why

they never took the risk to try."
Then slowly he clenched down to bite.
The smile on his face was slight.

His eyes were closed as in a dream
of happy things and things serene,

And slowly his eyes woke to see.
He turned and stared them right at me.

"Please tell Irene for me, kind sir,
her pickles are as good as her.

And really I can't say enough.
This is truly good and honest stuff."

So, "Happy Birthday, Irene!" Your goodness shows!
Zippity do da click-clack-close.

A Lost Art

It's "spring breakup," a period when logging activities shut down, giving the forest time to dry and loggers a well-deserved rest. Back in the day, it was celebrated with fanfare, large parties and relief since the timber harvest required exhausting and sometimes dangerous manual labor.

Still, for those who worked hard, the money was good. But to work hard, you needed a healthy chain saw. Mine wasn't.

It was late spring of 1972, and my chain saw wouldn't run. That was a problem because my father and I had begun work on a forty-acre timber sale and we had just two years to get it done. That may not sound difficult since a modern logging crew can do this work in a few days, but Dad had a small farm and a full-time job, while I had to juggle two years of high school, sports, fishing, hunting, a social life and of course, cleaning my room. It was my job to cut down, cut up and peel the trees—he'd skid them, pile them and arrange the trucking. So, just like the professional loggers (who didn't have to clean their rooms) with saw troubles, I did the reasonable thing and brought the saw to Jack Bort's Sturgeon Garage.

The garage was located southwest of Cook in Sturgeon Township. A quiet bedroom community now, it was a bustling place in the '70s with a general store, a bar, a café, a thrift shop and Jack's place. I walked into the shop as Jack stepped out from the back in his striped coveralls to greet me. I began telling him about the saw while he casually packed his pipe, giving an occasional "Hmmm," or "Uh huh," or "I see." Then he lit his pipe and in a cloud of smoke said, "Let's take a look." And back to his workbench we went.

This was where a stop at a small engine shop ended and a "Jack Bort experience" began. With pipe clenched in his teeth and screwdriver in hand, Jack began analyzing the saw while jumping waist-deep into political commentary, wandering between policies and politicians. He was well-read about the facts and didn't come across agitated or frustrated. Instead, he toyed with an issue much in the way a cat plays with a ball of yarn—batting it around a little, taking an occasional nip and generally enjoying the moment. Then he would finish with something like, "The wife and I were getting used to having clothes on our backs and food to eat, but the new tax code suggests we were being greedy." Or, "I was going to send a letter to Congress, but I didn't know which planet to send it to." And he'd laugh.

After a bit, he caught me off-guard by asking my opinion on a particular issue. It was a compliment that he bothered, but I hardly knew what a "politic" was, let alone have a valid opinion. I don't recall my response or if Jack even expected one, but it didn't matter. In a moment, he tugged on the starter rope and the saw jumped to life. He ran it full throttle, let it idle, then shut it down. "Good to go!" he said, and we were done. Thinking about it now, the cost to fix the saw was well worth the price of the show.

We had more discussions over the years and eventually I developed opinions of my own. We didn't always agree, but the conversation was always good. And apparently, the same held true for hundreds, maybe thousands, of other customers, since Jack's Sturgeon Garage was awarded for being number one in Jonsered chain saw sales in the U.S. in 1972. There is a lesson in that somewhere. I really need to go visit Jack for a cup of coffee again.

Mr. Personality 101

While each of us is quite unique, there are just four basic personality traits or tendencies. Understanding your personality is a fairly easy exercise, so let's view the four patterns that make up the whole of a person's personality. For clarity and for the fun of it, we'll also look at how these principles apply to a friend of mine, Donny.

The people in the first group of tendencies are referred to as communicators. Communicators are people-oriented, social, spontaneous, optimistic, high-energy, impulsive, flexible, curious, enthusiastic, influential and expressive. They want to be accepted, don't care much for details, get bored quickly, welcome new ideas and they love to help. My friend Don embodies the term "social." If gold bars fell out of the sky, rather than hoard them, he'd call up a bunch of folks to tell them what he found and invite them all to come pick gold bars with him—that is, if there would be any gold bars left after his long telephone call.

The second group is made up of the controllers. Controllers are decision makers who are direct, focused, tough, analytical, strategic, competitive, courageous, ambitious and not afraid to take risks. They're comfortable with authority, prestige and variety. They don't like to lose, they don't take criticism well and they're willing to beg forgiveness rather than seek permission in order to get things done. Don missed a huge buck about six years ago and he doesn't like it when his cousin Jim criticizes him about it. Don has been strategizing on a plan to get even with Jim. It's a risky plan that could backfire on him, but it's a risk he's willing to take.

The third group is the harmonizers. Harmonizers are team players who are loyal, supportive, patient, easygoing, stable, predictable, amiable and good listeners. They are uncomfortable with sudden change or unethical procedures. They like security and predictability. Sometimes they're too lenient, they avoid risk and they'll do anything for you if they feel appreciated. I was talking with some guys not long ago and one of them said, "You know, that Donny Aune sure is an amiable guy." We argued over that for a while but eventually agreed that Donny is amiable—a poor aim, maybe, but certainly amiable.

The fourth group is made up of the data specialists. Data specialists are accurate, persistent, analytical, precise, reserved and logical. They fear mistakes and criticism of their work so they tend to overanalyze. They are intuitive. They can appear aloof or unemotional and they're driven to do high-quality work, sometimes to the point of being called perfectionists. Last fall, I helped Donny build a deer stand and I'm here to tell you that his stand will outlive a chunk of granite. With attention to detail that rivals a Swiss watch, his 2,000-pound collection of cement, treated wood, coated nails, deck rails, pee pails, screws by the bales and ramparts overlooking trails is sure to eventually become the Wikipedia icon for "perfectionist" (even though it is illogical).

As you've noticed, Don exemplifies each personality trait to some extent, which is typical. We're each a mix of personality traits. Some may be 50% of one and 50% of another. Some may be 25%–25%–25%–25%. Some may be 90%–5%–5%–0%. There is no right or wrong, better or worse. Each mix can make for a great leader or each can make for a great kindergarten teacher. Those with a 90% mix of one trait are simply easier to identify. An interesting take is that some of these traits work better together as a team than others. For example, a controller and harmonizer make a great work team, as do a communicator and a data specialist. On the other hand, two communicators may come up with a lot of ideas but fail to follow through.

But it gets more complicated. Personality can be affected by your upbringing, environment, age, values, your birth order and your lot in life. And personality can change. Even surly old Ebenezer Scrooge changed once he realized what was truly important. I happen to be deficient in the area of data, which must have made my analytical father wonder where his impulsive son came from. It was no coincidence that as I relied on Dad for mechanical advice, I relied heavily, too, on the precision of our engineering team at work to better do my job. To complicate things even further, personalities can be kept under wraps due to cultural influences, shyness, anger, traumatic experiences or medical conditions. Here's something to think about: strengths are good, but if you don't realize the weaknesses your personality presents in certain situations you run the risk of thinking you're always right.

Indeed, it takes all kinds of people to make this world tick and each is as important as the next. Some of the best committees I've been on included all of the personality traits at the table. It's great when a communicator has a big idea, while a data specialist warns where the idea could fail, while a harmonizer supports the merits of both thoughts, as a controller tries to figure out how to make it all work. Indeed, variety is the spice of life, but don't take my word for it. Ask Don. Just allow yourself plenty of time for an answer.

Look, Mom!

Mother's Day is on the horizon, and it takes place on the same weekend as Minnesota's opening day of fishing. The mixing of these two events is unfortunate and mothers, patient as they are, usually don't offer much complaint. It seems they deserve more undivided attention than they get because that's what they specialize in—giving others their undivided attention. My mother was a great example. Whatever the achievement, whatever the mess, she was always there for me.

Mom waited on me hand and foot after my surgery. And when all that attention started me on a path of temper tantrums she'd splash a little water on my head, which "cured" me instantly. She was on hand to provide first aid after Dad pushed me and my bike down a hill to teach me how to ride. She kept an eye on me when I ran away from home, all the way to the far side of the pasture. And she rescued me after I created a chemical stew of cleaning agents, which smoked and sizzled in a caustic brew that threatened to burn down our house. All of this before I turned six.

When I was a growing boy, Mom would put a big piece of dessert on my plate even when I complained I was stuffed and couldn't eat another bite. She'd say, "Oh, you don't have to eat it, just try it," which implied there was a significant difference. She, not my dad, taught me the facts of life, which wasn't so tough when living on a farm. And when things didn't go well, Mom would always assure me that things would work out.

There was one time, though, when I was about twelve, that her loving support was a fearsome thing. The Swanson boys and I rode our bikes down to the rapids to try some fishing one summer morning, but the next thing you know it was afternoon and I was a couple miles down the road hanging out with another friend, Gordy. By evening, I was five miles down the road eating popcorn with the Anderson boys, when a car pulled into the yard driven by Mom, who feared her son (the one who hadn't called home) had drowned at the rapids. It was the only time I saw my mother unhinged. She was half crazy with anger and relief, but I knew she had gone bonkers for all the right reasons. My keen survival instincts learned growing up on a dead-end road told me I shouldn't tell her she was silly for worrying. I just took it and hoped she wouldn't kill me.

Despite this and other foolish stunts on my part, Mom continued to support me any way she could. During my senior year in high school, she had made steaks for supper the night before a basketball game with Albrook High. That game happened to be the best night of my high school career and Mom claimed full responsibility for it by virtue of the steak supper. You'll never guess what she cooked for supper every night before Friday games for the rest of the season. Yeah. It was good times.

As memorable as anything, Mom laughed often and talked a lot, which worked out great because Dad was a man of few words. She liked to joke that she wore a size seven shoe, "but the nines feel so good." A quirk she had was to closely follow the travels of various viruses in the neighborhood, of which she was sure she had symptoms. In reality, she was healthy as a horse most of the time. Her chatter about us, the news, the neighbor's whereabouts, the weather and her plans for the week was music to our ears, but we really didn't realize that at the time. One Thanksgiving Day she stood up at the table for the only speech I ever remember her giving. We were all there. She said that she had lived a full life, she was proud of us and she had no regrets. That was about it. She died a month later on Christmas morning, and we soon came to realize how much we'd miss her rambling chatter at the table. It created a quiet at our little farm that took years to get used to.

Wishing they were both still here, I can imagine visiting with Mom at the kitchen table while waiting for Dad to come in from the garage for morning coffee. I would bring her some fish fillets and might have said, "Hey, Mom, I'm doing some writing." And she probably would go into a long story about how I used to like to fish at the river when I was little and she always figured I'd write something and Grandpa was a writer, too, and the neighbors were on vacation again and she thought she was coming down with the same bug her friend Ann had and I wouldn't really have had to say anything more until it was time to go. But it would be a great conversation and I'd feel good even though I knew she would say those things even before she said them. Then she'd put another biscuit on my plate while I would complain about being full and couldn't eat another bite and she'd say, "Oh, you don't have to eat it. Just try it."

And I would. I'd eat the whole thing just to make her feel good.

Grandpa John

My grandfather John came to America at the turn of the century on the Carpathia, a ship that years later would come to the aid of survivors of the sunken Titanic. He was the only member of his family of six siblings to immigrate, which left him quite alone as a young man in a new country. When he stepped off the boat in New York, did he have a plan? How, I ask, does a person of modest means go from there? Was he excited about making a new life or racked with doubt? What prepares a twenty-year-old for such a challenge?

Most of the men in John's family were either tailors or policemen, but through some unknown set of events, he established a farming life in northern Minnesota, which is not an easy thing to do. No, let's be more specific about that—it's a seemingly impossible thing to do. Using horse and hands, he cleared sixty acres of forest that was situated fifteen rugged miles from the nearest town. He constructed a home, barn, sheds and sauna and somehow raised money to purchase livestock. Along the way, he took a wife and started a family. For fun he did some boxing, taught gymnastics, played baritone in a band and served also as the band conductor. For extra income, he would custom butcher for neighbors and eventually he even managed to buy a brand-new Ford. If you knew the "inside story" on my grandfather you'd know he was a poor farmer, meaning he was not good at it. His side interests took away from precious time in the field and his ways caused arguments between he and my grandmother, Hanna. He was a poor judge of horses and the farm paid the price that extolled. He wasn't a great builder, either, as testified by shoddy foundations that led to the demise of nearly all he had built within a decade of his passing at the age of sixty. But far from diminishing his memory, I hold these things about my Grandpa John, a man I never knew, with respect. He was either fearless, confident, adventurous, lucky or maybe all four. He may not have been a good farmer but he did it. He maintained a passion for sports and music even though it must surely have sacrificed at least some of his prosperity. He came to the US with almost nothing, but he left on this earth a family who mourned, a home in the woods, friends, neighbors, a nice Ford, grandchildren and future grandchildren who think about him still.

Sometimes I think too much is made of heritage. Oh, it's interesting enough. Physical features of ancestors, the history of how we got here and the like. And now, DNA can even show the potential of avoiding health concerns before they surface. But heritage in itself does not ensure status or value, as has been unjustly upheld through history. Indeed, ancestors can pass down a legacy of knowledge or love but each of us needs to make our own way. If I'm related to a pharaoh, so what?

More intriguing to me are the untold stories of people who must have helped my grandfather to accomplish all he did, but I am left to guess about that. And I can only hope to do as well in contributing as Grandpa did. The thought turns me again to the caption under my senior picture in a Cook High School annual: "I don't know where I am going, but I'm on my way." These words, chosen at random, yet internalized, have guided me, sometimes haphazardly, through many avenues in my life, but it wasn't until this morning that I realized that these same words likely spoke to the way my Grandpa John lived his. There were times he could not know the outcomes of his actions and he had limitations, but he carried on. I relate to that. Labor Day came and went yet again without the fanfare it once held, but it's still good to remember how others broke trail for us. Technology gets all the press nowadays and indeed, it's a nice tool, but it's our labor that gets things done. There must be a moral in that somewhere.

Remembering Roy

A sultry summer day long ago found me high in a white spruce tree, enjoying the view for a deer stand I planned to build at a later date. Ominous rumblings warned of an approaching storm from the west, causing me to think, *One more of those and I'm getting out of this tree*, but at the present, I was fixated on finding the right spot for the stand. In what seemed only a minute or two, a tremendous CRACK BALOOM exploded in the forest around me as a simultaneous flash indicated the strike was close. I skittered down that tree like a squirrel on fire, then ran full tilt all the way back to the safety of the house. I never want to be that close to lightning again.

You probably haven't heard of a strapping man from the state of Virginia named Roy Sullivan. Roy worked as a United States park ranger from 1942 to 1977, and he earned a place in the Guinness Book of World Records as the person to be struck by lightning more than anyone else: seven times! It's a title we are all too glad to let him own. Roy was struck in almost every way one can come in contact with lightning, which includes: directly, the most deadly; a side flash, where lightning strikes an object and then jumps to a victim nearby; ground currents, where lightning hits an object (usually a tree), which in turn energizes nearby ground (this is the most common way to be electrocuted by lightning); and conduction, in which lightning hits a structure and then travels through conductive metal, wiring or plumbing to the victim.

It didn't help that Roy posted duty in a fire tower without lightning protection in the lightning-prone state of Virginia, a fact that accounted for his first contact, but that was not the scene of every strike. He was struck in his truck as he drove down the road, again while working in a garage, another time out in his yard, again while fishing, once while cutting wheat on a farm and yet again, standing outside his truck while on routine patrol. He had holes burned in his appendages. His hair, eyebrows and eyelashes had been burned off in separate incidents and he suffered numerous electrical burns in other parts of his body. Understandably, Roy lived the latter part of his life fearing that he was cursed in some unusual way. And he wasn't the only one who believed this—many folks in the area avoided him for fear of becoming lightning victims as well.

When I first heard of Roy's story, comedic scenes came to mind reminiscent of the Road Runner cartoon show, where the coyote suffers one catastrophic event after another as he keeps coming back, vigorously trying to catch his dinner. But of course, that was just a cartoon. A very sad aside to this story is that after surviving seven strikes, Roy eventually ended his own life—a life that history suggests became lonely due to his "bad luck." It makes me wonder if anyone tried to comfort Roy in his worries over curses or to understand what it was like to be in his shoes. Or did he only receive passing comments such as, "You're one tough guy, Roy!" or "I hope you don't mind if I sit over here, Roy. Ha! Ha!"

There are takeaways from Roy's story. First, lightning takes too many lives and it's often due to people hesitating to seek shelter when storms approach. I wish I had a dollar for every time a fisherman sat in the middle of the bay near our cabin with lightning all about but refused to leave until the rain started. (Wouldn't want to get wet, you know.) Maybe it's just me, but having millions of volts of electricity coursing through the body should be more concerning than getting wet. Whatever, it's a free country. And just like lightning, suicide takes too many lives and it's often due to people hesitating to seek shelter when life's "storms" approach. Are we watching? Do we listen for signs of trouble? A person shouldn't need to be figuratively hit by lightning before receiving help beyond Band-Aids. Life is difficult and it always has been, but it's worth the trouble. The signs of depression, sadness or despair can be subtle, and rare is the individual who has not lived with these feelings at least for a time. Seek shelter. Provide shelter. Life is good. Remember Roy.

Mighty Marvin

If, in the summary of a person's life, the words used to define it are: honest, kind, nice and caring, the life was special indeed. That was Marvin Aune. I had the good fortune of working with and being a friend to Marvin, who, sadly, left us. The poem below was written twenty years ago in honor of Marv's retirement. With changes in the wording and blessing of the family, this is again respectably submitted in his honor.

Mighty Marvin

Once upon a distant time in the little town of Cook,
A town like Casey's Mudville with an "up north" kind of look,
There lived a man named Marvin who was working on the rails.
A man of fun and daring and yes, a man of many tales.
To be a man of many tales means you must play many roles.
So, Marv said "bye" to ties and rocks and started climbing poles.
But when he told his family of the deed that he had done,
His dad said, "Man, you're crazy!" His mom just said, "Strike one!"
Undaunted, Marvin took the job with vigorous embrace.
A determination hidden on his kind, endearing face.
But shortly after hiring on, his hopes were quickly dashed.
The work had slowed up plenty, so the work force was then slashed.
Some men took it hard, they say, for work they had to wish.

Marvin simply took the time to hunt and trap and fish.
He reasoned, "I'm just twenty-eight. I can work to sixty-two."
But somewhere back within in his mind, his mother said, "Strike two!"
Things got back to normal with Marv back on the job.
He worked all hours upon the line until his ankles throbbed.
He worked with Harold, Don and Bud and Edgar, Jack and Phil.
With the Cheneys and Jim Tesson and Arnie, Butch and Bill.
And while he dealt with these guys he took time to find a wife.
Her name was Linda Tokvam; she was the center of his life.
And soon enough came Dawn and George and little Timothy,
And Linda's pitch to Marvin was: Tim will be "Strike three!"
And unbeknownst to most around, Marv liked to flirt with danger.
He killed a black bear off his porch, rode thin ice with his Ranger.
He was great at playing baseball, smashed a boat upon the rocks,
He worked daily on high voltage and he never got a shock.
But there's so much more to Marvin than the antics that we've heard.
And no, it's not his "gift of gab," but the wisdom of his word.
The famous men of history on which we've been well-schooled
Were men of dash and daring and men who overruled.
Men who won great battles, like MacArthur, Grant and Lee
Or brothers Wright who overcame the laws of gravity.
"What's this to do with Marv?" you ask, who's not in any book.
If you never saw his wisdom, then you simply didn't look!
Ask Marv and he'd say "Maybe," or at best, "I don't think so."
For wisdom is the knowledge that there's so much more to know.
The world could use more "Marvins" who sit happily on the fence
Too often we're ruled by opinions instead of common sense.
So, sadly do we say "goodbye" to Marv—he was the best.
Yet, still we're glad our little town is where he made his nest.
Retiring to his lofty island, Marv surely is in glory
Leaving every person that he knew a favorite Marvin story.
And if you listen 'round the town, you'll likely hear the tout,
"You know, it just ain't been the same since Mighty Marv checked out."

King of Basketball

It was a basketball game between the Cook Little Gophers and the Orr Braves on the Braves' home court, where I found myself hopelessly trapped in a half-court press. It felt more like being caught in a half nelson in a wrestling match—only worse. Coach Hokkanen called a time-out to bail me out and as our team huddled up to discuss yet again how we might break the press, I looked over and saw Coach King "actively" admonishing the Braves players and generally making it quite clear to anyone in the gym that whatever it was that displeased him would not be tolerated. Now, this is just a guess on my part, but had the situation been reversed and we had a suffocating press along with a good lead on the Braves, we would have been sharing back slaps and party favors during the time-out. Of course, I jest, but it's probably safe to say our expectations did not match theirs.

Demanding and high expectations is the Bill King way, and it is the way of excellent coaches I've come to know over the years. Basketball is not that complicated, but it's hard work if done correctly. Yes, the game requires specific skills, but if players aren't dedicated to giving a total effort to the common cause it can be reduced to not much above organized exercise. So, when Bill gave his boys the business for holding a ten-point lead, it was because he knew they should have had a twenty-point lead. Every possession should make sense. No lead allows "freebie" shots for the fun of it. Each defensive effort should be intense and every player aware of the responsibility.

I still play some basketball and many of the fellows who show up to the gym are from Orr and Nett Lake. And even though some of them are in their forties and fifties, they'll still comment after making a bad decision, "Don't tell Coach King what I just did!" or "Uh-oh, Coach is going to bench me for that one." It's always good for a laugh and it brings back good memories of experiences gone by. I never even played for the guy but I'll use the same lines. Watching Bill King chastising his players that night back in '72, I specifically remember thinking it must be tough playing for a guy like that. But it stayed with me and I ended up doing some coaching myself, and I get it now.

It's been my good fortune to have been part of a great football team, experiencing the explosiveness and grit that went with it. I have a warm spot for baseball, especially the skills, the strategies and the intermittent leisure the game allows. But basketball is a passion which, when done properly, strikes me as an art form of sorts. I've said it before: even great-grandma who has never seen a game before would appreciate good basketball (hustle, precision, skill, awareness) when she sees it. Bill King's teams were like that. I can't say I know Bill well, but as often happens in the northland, we all seem to know each other to some extent. I recall meeting Coach King on the street when I was still a player and it was clear he recognized who I was and he acknowledged me. I took that as a compliment. And while playing against him was frustrating more often than not, it feels now like an honor. Living legends have such an effect. Given this, it goes without saying that the Orr Braves weren't the only ones to benefit from Coach King, or "Billy King" as most folks of his generation like to refer to him. I'm just not sure if I have the right to do that. And after being stuck in his half nelson, half-court press, I'd rather not do anything to be in a situation of being "against" him again because I'm here to tell you– you don't want to be there.

Treat Yourself

The seat on my aging tractor is similar to the steel seats found on old horse-drawn farm implements. A key difference is that when the tractor was new, the seat had a firm, molded cushion built in that gave the warmth and security of sitting in a good saddle. But time, water and weather eventually did their damage, and the once-comfy ride was now down to cold bare metal. Yeah, sit on that for a while.

So, I stepped into Hongisto Implement, located in Cloquet, a few years ago and as usual, Jim Hongisto was behind the counter, which was behind the rack of leaf springs, which was behind the rack of cultivator parts. Getting right to the point, I asked Jim if he had tractor seat covers and just as quickly he replied in his slow, low voice, "Over there," pointing to a large rack of parts up against a side wall.

There it was: second shelf from the bottom, a red-and-white vinyl seat cover wrapped in plastic. Anyone who has an old tractor will attest that it's fun to see a hint of what their tractor looked like forty or fifty or sixty years ago, because after so much time most tractors become camouflaged in a mix of dull paint, rust, grease and mud. Gauges, if there are any, are cloudy and broken and there are holes in places where parts used to be. Anyway, I asked, "Will it fit my Farmall 404?" Jim said, "Yup." Turning the piece over showed a price tag of twenty dollars. I couldn't believe my good luck and how talkative Jim was that day, but it was time to check out. Then it happened.

While pulling out my wallet, my gaze was redirected to yet another rack (Jim was fond of keeping all of his inventory where he could see it), on which I saw… or I thought it was… could it be? It was a brand-spanking-new original-equipment cushioned seat! Eyes wide open, I asked, "Does that seat fit a 404 too?" "Yup," he said. I walked over and picked it up. It was hefty and beautiful, leather and steel, deep red and cool white and I knew that you don't find one of these things on any street corner. But knowing also how original parts are gilded in gold and held in highest esteem by pawn shops and the banking industry, I said apprehensively, "Suppose it's kind of expensive, huh?" In an uncompromising tone, Jim replied, "Hunnerd bucks." "A hundred bucks?" I quizzed, resigning myself to the fact that the cheap cover was "good enough." With a parting gaze, I moved to put the seat back onto the shelf and as I did, Jim, in his direct and dry-as-a-desert-wind manner said, "Treat yourself." I could be wrong, but he may have actually been smiling. Soon, I was smiling, too, and you know what? I bought that crazy seat. Best thing I ever did—well, a good thing anyway.

Be assured, I have not gone over the deep end in promoting purchasing as a path to happiness. But doggone it, it's important to treat yourself once in a while without feeling guilty and I owe Jim Hongisto much thanks for his "lesson in twelve words or less." All I can say is that the new seat feels so good I can't even explain it—if only my backside could talk. Well, you know what I mean.

CHAPTER 4: LESSONS

What Life is Telling Me

She Won't Mow the Daisies

The year is 2217 on the planet Saturn. A guy steps into a restaurant and tells the waitress, "I'd like a moon mist with a twist please." The waitress says, "Sure thing. By the way, you wouldn't happen to be from Earth, would you?" The guy replies, "Yes, I am. Why do you ask?" The waitress offers, "It's your accent. You sound like my husband's relatives from Earth." "No kidding?" says the patron. "Where on Earth was your husband from?" "Oh, you wouldn't know the place," she replies. "His family runs a little business in the central wilderness of North America called Kettle Falls Hotel." "That's unbelievable!" exclaims the patron, "I have friends in Orr, a metro nearby, and we take hydrofoils to Kettle Falls every couple of years. You should come with us next time!" And such is the start of another friendship on the planet Saturn.

Just like this chance encounter on Saturn, I've come to notice that when traveling or in unfamiliar surroundings, people look for a connection with other people. A connection may be that you and a stranger are simply both from the US. Better yet if you're both from the Midwest or even Orr, Minnesota. Maybe a common interest is kids or black labs or some other shared experience and these things seem to confirm a phrase that has been getting traction in the news lately, which is, "We have much more in common than we have differences."

Testing this theory a few days ago, our party of ten traveled forty miles by water across Crane, Sand Point and Namakan Lakes to a remote hotel-restaurant-bar on the US/Canadian border called Kettle Falls Hotel. Meet our crew: Bob is tall and born in Iowa, which was handy when the conversation turned to corn. His wife, Candyce, collects rocks and is not from Iowa. Charlie is a former Marine who once destroyed a propeller on his boat while navigating Lake Superior—not an easy thing to do. Linda, wife of Charlie Shipwreck, is a former co-worker of mine. Ben and Tania love popcorn and would have gladly trolled for walleyes for forty miles along the way. Jeff, a cliff jumper from the Cherry/Zim area and my daughter, Beth, served as chaperones. My wife, Lindy "Is that a Rock?" Wilenius, was the navigator.

Once at the hotel, we were among strangers. We met a disheveled canoeist who had traveled 4,000 miles and really needed someone to talk to. Some folks asked where we were from, others donated chairs for our table, one knew my neighbor and the Canadians there didn't try to argue whether hockey is better than basketball. I suppose we could have stuck around and tried to ferret out a person's politics or their religion or their opinion on hockey and argue about it, but we didn't. Really, why would we? Everyone there just enjoyed the day, oblivious of differences. The boat trip and my experiences of traveling in general remind me of another lesson, this one learned from my lawn.

To explain, my wife and I get along pretty well, but we disagree on some things, not the least of which is our lawn. When it comes to mowing, I am from the school of "take no prisoners." Any blade of grass, dandelion, poplar sapling or emerging anthill crazy enough to grow beyond three inches or so will be leveled by my powerful, dull lawnmower in the interest of symmetry. It is the way a lawn is supposed to look: even, clean boundaries and thoroughly cut. My wife, on the other hand, negotiates with our lawn. She can be found standing with the mower running while a bug waddles out of the way. She moves things that I simply mulch for fertilizer. And crazily enough, she won't mow the daisies. If there happens to be a lone daisy along the sidewalk or seven in a bunch in the middle of the lawn, she leaves them be. It's an irritation but I've come to respect the little critters on her account.

Simply put, for forty years we have agreed to disagree once in a while and neither of us gave up our values. Navigating is more important than winning. It would be nice to see more folks, even politicians, get realistic and work on places where they can agree or agree to disagree where necessary instead of throwing their differences around like hand grenades. We have more things in common than not, with the exception of those folks from Mars, because I think we can all agree that those Martians are incorrigible. But that's beside the point.

It's also safe to say that all Earthlings (not just Americans) have much in common because almost all people—whether in China, Kenya, Iraq, North Korea or Lichtenstein—want the same things we do: a home, food, friends, safety, a future for their children, happiness, a boat ride to Kettle Falls once in a while and a well-manicured lawn without daisies. Ha!

Heroes and Villains

Breakfast was cooking when a fellow being interviewed on television commented, "We are both the heroes and villains in our own lives." The statement caught my attention, so I shut down the oatmeal to hear more. Was this profound insight or just nifty play on words to impress the audience? I had to know.

Before getting an answer, the program went on to another topic, but with a little web research I soon had the answer and you know what? It's true. According to Dan McAdams, a Northwestern University psychologist, our life experiences produce lasting impressions on us—good and bad. Experiences help form and define us, but it is the stories we tell ourselves about these experiences, or our "internal narratives," as he calls them, that are more important than the facts themselves. As he summarizes, "Our narrative identity has heroes and villains that can help us or hold us back, major events that determine the plot, challenges overcome and suffering we have endured."

To put this in practice, let's say a fellow capsizes a canoe in a crashing surf on Minnesota's sprawling Lake Vermilion. From this, he may be forever grateful to have survived and is inspired to give back to society. Or he might realize an inner strength that helps him become a leader who relishes challenge. Or he may be severely traumatized and never want to be that close to walleyes again. Or he could feel angry and victimized because nobody warned him about the adverse relationship between sweeping Niles Bay and canoeing. There is much more to the topic, but the short story is that internal heroes are the positive stories you tell yourself that help you to grow, while villains are the negative stories that limit you. I can go along with that.

But what defines the heroes and villains that fill the evening news? Instead of looking this one up on the internet, I'm going rogue and will share some random thoughts. I think we make too many heroes of people we don't know and villains of people we don't understand. There can be dishonest, self-serving people in positions of prominence as well as mistaken but caring, generous hearts in trouble with the law. I offer the utmost respect for thousands but hold my hero cards close to my chest. If almost everyone is a hero, that leaves only me and a couple of my deadbeat buddies as the fan club. Superman is a great guy, and maybe he is a hero because he's faster than a speeding bullet and he can save the world without breaking a sweat, however, if he didn't do heroic things, his mother would whack him alongside the head. He does what he should do lest he surrender his talents to another who would use them better. I'm just glad he didn't go to the dark side.

My soft spot is for another group sometimes referred to as "everyday heroes," who do their thing quietly and without recognition. The northland happens to be lousy with them—people who volunteer, encourage, support, guide, advocate, fix and befriend by putting a piece of themselves out there. One story on that: twenty-some years ago, a boy was riding home on a school bus. Across the aisle older boys relentlessly bullied a small girl, maybe only eight years old, till she began to cry. The boy told the bullies to stop and predictably, his action drew the abuse from the girl to himself. It was a brave thing to do for a ten-year-old without superpowers. After a long bus ride home, the boy, Dave never said a word about the incident and it was some time later that his sister, Beth told me about what happened. Maybe it's not my place to call Dave or Beth, heroes since they're my kids, but they do good things. In fact, most people I've come to know do very good things. You probably do, as well. So, tell yourself some good stories about you. You deserve it.

We sure covered a lot of ground from making oatmeal, didn't we?

Coffee Break

The break room at work was small but it held two tables, which, by ten in the morning, were filled to capacity, typically with women at one table and men at the other. It was the early 1980s and the atmosphere was loud with conversation, making it feel as if more people were talking than listening. Outbursts of laughter were deafening as thick smoke filled whatever space was not taken up by the tightly packed dozen or more people engaged there. Boy, those were the days.

The coffee breaks were rich with variety and deep with insights on all kinds of things: child rearing, travel, fixing things, movies, sports, cars, work issues, funny stories, tragic stories, recipes, fishing tips, rumors, marriage counseling and even politics, to name a few. It's quite an honor to be allowed into the personal experiences of others. With such exchanges, you could understand why someone felt as they did, because you knew them. You knew the names of their children and their hobbies and their foibles. What was special was that people of different ages, disciplines, ranks and interests gathered into one conversation with no distractions and truly listened to each other. And if I had a story or opinion to contribute to the conversation, it would be heard by the group in turn. Other than smoke-induced tears, it was great to belong. And the camaraderie developed there led to ski weekends, Twins games, snowmobile trips and picnics after work hours.

Thirty years later and just prior to my retirement, coffee breaks, for the most part, had become a different animal. Most visible—or more appropriately, not visible—was that the air in the break room was clear, with smoking having since been moved outside. But the crowd was gone too. Nine o'clock might find a person on break glued to their phone. Nine fifteen with two or three friends in discussion. Nine thirty might have a random collection of folks, some on phones, some reading the paper and a couple others in dialogue. By ten, the last few coffee drinkers dribbled in and out, many of whom would simply fill their cups and retreat back to their desks with their phones. At times, I fit into any one of those scenarios. The point is, the coffee break just wasn't what it used to be, and seldom did a dozen people share a conversation anymore.

Are we not as socially adjusted as the generations before

us? Or can we simply place blame on the distractions of technology? There is no doubt that technology allows for a lot of contacts, but I jump on the bandwagon that argues it does not make for the same investment in conversation, friendship and understanding like it was back in the days of sitting across the table from others, where respect and manners mattered. One comment I've heard on technology goes, "Social media today allows people to act like first graders." Well, from my experience, that's not being fair to first graders. Take a trip to your local school if you don't believe me. Those kids are respectful and they play with each other... and their hands and faces are sticky.

The point is not that we need crowded, smoke-filled rooms to get back to honest and informative dialogue, but then again, who knows? Maybe we do. At least we'd be at the table. If you're a member of a group that can talk about a lot of things, good for you! You're a member of a dying breed... or else a first grader.

Sunset

Our story begins in the spring of 1996, in the backyard of a neighbor, where the distress calls of one very hungry orphaned fawn (mother deceased nearby) alerted the neighbor, who took the little critter in and successfully pulled it back from the brink of death in the warmth of his home.

As the deer got older, it began hanging out at the nearby corner store where "other people" were, and in the effort to make new friends it would greet those who came to shop. It was a unique experience. One day I pulled up to the gas pumps and watched as a mother with young son in hand came around the corner of the store only to be surprised by the deer standing at the top of the steps. Mother and son were taken aback, as one might expect, and after the initial encounter they slipped past the deer and on to their shopping. It was a "Kodak moment," as they say.

That fall, a friend and neighbor was walking to his deer stand in an adjacent wood on opening morning. Once getting to his stand he realized he had company—the neighborhood deer. Now, this strikes me as a great decoy opportunity for bringing in a big buck, but having a deer hanging out under his stand was distracting enough (or maybe dangerous enough) to have him conclude, "Oh what's the use?" He headed home with the deer trailing close behind; he'd hunt another day. Picturing the thought of a hunter on stand with a deer loitering under it makes for laughs around local campfires still.

The next year on a beautiful night in September, we passed by the community town hall on a drive home and saw a neighbor kid, Dan Swanson, shooting hoops at the basketball court, as he did much of the time. Our car was still moving as we pulled up to our house when Patrick, our youngest, opened the back door and jumped out, saying, "I'm going down to the court to shoot with Dan!" and just like that, he was on his bike and gone. Later, my wife and I took an evening walk to the court, where the boys were in a heated game of one-on-one. It was always that way with the two friends when a basketball was involved—intense, faces red, skin glistening with sweat, shots blocked and bodies colliding, only this time a white-tailed deer was in the mix. The boys seemed to care little about the deer's presence one way or another as they occasionally bumped into it and even used it as a screen for a move to the basket.

The deer took leave from the game to greet us, sniffing our faces until, having enough of that, I yelled out, "It's getting late, you boys better get home soon," and we left for our walk back. We had gone just a short distance when a sound caught our attention. Turning around to look, we spotted a small flock of Canadian geese settling low over the court as they prepared to land in the adjacent field. Framing that, the brilliant sunset painted a scattering of clouds in glows of yellow, orange and red. Wrapped within, a deer and two young boys—two close friends and two close neighbors—competed desperately, unaware of the spectacle that surrounded them.

The picture from that night is priceless, but it is only in my mind. To recreate such a scene would take the brilliant colors of a Terry Redlin painting, the charm of a Norman Rockwell, the perfect timing of photographer Jim Brandenburg and of course, the boys and a deer. But the boys (and the deer) are no longer with us. Losing a child is an experience that strips a person to the core and redefines everything going forward. It makes the memory from that evening on the basketball court both difficult and a blessing at the same time. And I miss the pictures that would have been had life gone on.

If heaven allows, I believe the boys are playing basketball still. And there must be other players and friends there, and some people are cheering or some are visiting in the stands, or maybe some are there just for the popcorn. Why not? All I know is that my faith dictates there can't be a beautiful sunrise without a sunset first. This promise and those around us today make for a changed but blessed life that wasn't expected. I've seen the sunset. The sunrise to come is more than I can imagine.

 **RETIREMENT**

Lessons from the Little Big Horn

The question "Should I retire?" is difficult to advise since situations are unique and in the end we must each decide for ourselves. It's going well for me. The following poem is not meant to be a guide to retirement, but if it gives you something to think about it, then it wasn't a complete waste of your time, eh?

She Won't Mow the Daisies

For most of your life you have worked hard and
long to provide for your needs and your goals,

And sometimes you work hard to just get along
mending fences and patching up holes.

No one said your life would be easy or that years
would fly by without mention.

Now your stomach becomes kind of queasy when
your friends talk of health care and pension.

For there's comfort in schedules that fill out your
day and make weekends a thing that you treasure,

And the work is fulfilling; you make it that way
and it's part of your brand and your measure.

So, if you delight in the trail that you make and
still treasure the fruits of your labor,

Then please don't retire for retirement's sake, and
continue the quest that you savor.

'Cause the world needs more people who love what
they do—it produces great things and great work.

And maybe you work with a wonderful crew,
except for one guy who's a jerk.

But if retiring now from your hard-earned career is
a question continually nagging,

And your energy level feels like it's been robbed
and your stiff upper lip is now sagging,

And you're tired of living in front of a screen or
working in hot or cold weather,

And you're tired of "giving one up for the team" or
you feel like your job is a tether,

Leo Wilenius

Take heed in the notion that you're not alone, for
others have shown us a way.

Just put down your "do list" and shut off the
phone and hear now what I have to say.

To all who will listen, I'm not preaching to you,
just a story, you don't have to believe it.

For retiring is often a hard thing to do, it's your
living and it's hard to leave it.

But history can show us what's bad and what's
good so we refer to the story of Custer.

Who, instead of his taking time off as he should,
he took all of the men he could muster.

Sharply focused, he rode off and thought to himself, One more victory—I'm a national wonder!

Not a dusty old general stowed away on a shelf.
Yes, one last victory to add to my plunder.

Then he and his army trotted up to a stream, beyond it a village caught napping.

He ordered a "Charge!" with a yelp and a scream,
as he urged his horse on with a strapping.

A huge battle took shape and after a bit his sharp
focus proceeded to roam.

His hair was a mess, his left arm had been hit and
his right flank was heading for home.

So, he scrambled to a knoll with the last of his
men, then oddly, he sat down to write.

His captain rang out, "Sir, we're now down to ten.
Would you please drop your pen and help fight?"

Still, Custer just sat there; perhaps now he knew
that his idea of right was all wrong.

And he never took time for himself and his crew—
it was clear now he'd waited too long.

And perhaps he could see that the people he
fought only wanted some peace and a home,

For the misguided notion of justice he sought left
them no place to dream or to roam.

Yes, he was up to his armpits in gators, up a creek
in a boat with no paddle.

He was wading chest-deep in hip waders. All he
had left: a spent gun and a saddle.

The stories that last from the battle that day mostly
speak of his last shot at glory.

But here's a small fact, as Paul Harvey would say,
that lets you in on the rest of the story.

Custer's writings were found near his side, slightly
strewn, his pencil still clutched in his hand.

Some guessed he'd been writing the words for a
tune. In fact, it was his last command.

Twelve little words with his name signed above it.
If only he'd have done it before.

He wrote: "Take this job and shove it. I ain't working here no more."

So, I hope that the moral of this story is clear, and
friends, it's not meant to be tragic.

Rejoice in the good times of your working years
and if you choose to, retirement is magic.

You can go somewhere, help someone, read a
good book, it's no place for self-pity or sorrow.

You can learn to change oil or learn how to cook,
take your time, for there's always tomorrow.

It's a brand-new green pasture, go on, have a ball,
in a field that is yours if selected.

You can leave with thanksgivings from each one
and all and leave while you're still well-respected.

Goodbye and good luck and good tidings, good
friend, when you head off to please your own heart.

And remember that this time does not mark an
end, but instead, it's one glorious start.

Go on. Get outta there!

Wood Ducks

At the cabin a few years back, I woke up, started coffee
and hit the couch to wait as it brewed. It was only 5:00 a.m.
Looking through a window into the woods next door, a motion high in the trees caught my eye. It was a wood duck returning to its nest in a hollowed poplar tree. It was something
to witness, since they come in rather hot for the landing and
don't exactly hover like other tree-nesting birds. This partic-

ular nest was nearly forty feet up. If you know about wood ducks, you know that as soon as all the eggs in the clutch are hatched, the mother, in an act of tough love, flies away and encourages her babies (who must also think they can fly) to jump. Nature's plan is for the fluffy little critters to crash to the ground, bounce off the leaf litter below then join up with their anxiously awaiting mother. Strangely enough, the system works. Still, I couldn't help but wince thinking about the flight path this brood would encounter. Oh, there was leaf litter, all right—if you could get to it. There was also an almost impenetrable maze of broken trees, uprooted stumps, branches, rocks and brush that could stop a bulldozer. But that's nature for you. Chaotic debris, which is an obstacle for humans, is "descent control" and protective cover to a baby duck. It makes a point: nature loves chaos.

In the grand scheme of things, nature creates plenty of chaos through floods, drought, windstorms, fire, disease and other natural forces. These sometimes cause vast destruction, wiping out much, if not all incumbent life in an area. However, it also begins a vibrant change in the variety of habitat, plant types, food sources and even the lay of the land. If nature had its way, much of our northland would be cleansed by massive fires routinely. A micro example of natural chaos is the work of the beaver, whose dams kill out large areas of forest, which is unfortunate for resident plant and animal inhabitants. However, the process quickly provides new "edge" cover, water habitats and nutritious food sources where there were formerly few.

We (mankind) like variety, too, but we don't care for chaos because we don't do well in it. Instead, we work hard to manage it. We build stout shelters from the elements. We control floods. We domesticate plants and animals because wildlife is tough to catch and blueberries can have a bad year. We manage forests for fire control, wood production and wildlife. Of course, we fail at times in some of these efforts, but we progress, and even do quite well overall.

A new chaos provider we hear quite a bit about nowadays is climate change. Some feel it is a natural cycle, and perhaps some aspects of it are. However, eighty years ago scientists began recording noticeable changes in temperatures and pollutants in the atmosphere, and these concerned them. And if I trust science to perform surgery, fly me across oceans, create medicines to cure ills and build miraculous bridges that take us safely across deep chasms, but will not trust science to understand weather measurements, then I'm not being consistent. So, if it concerns them, it concerns me.

I don't know what happens if ocean currents divert or dwindling snow in the mountains stops feeding the mighty Missouri River, but if it is something we can fix, it will be a big task, and if it is not, it will be an even bigger task. Each option requires that we gear up to prepare. My choice to lead preparations for either condition is the science field because they study everything, not just trendy things. Second choice would be the military as they are serious folks and are already planning for the effects and possible conflicts due to climate change. Third, my sentimental favorite for the job would be the Minnesota Twins coaching staff because they want to win. Fourth choice is a coalition of young mindpower from various colleges since we may need new ideas and their youthful exuberance would likely make solutions fun at the same time. That's it. Politicians would serve only to carry out whatever plans one of these groups comes up with, because this is not the place for their opinion or mine.

Regardless of what we people do, wood ducks will continue to do well as they drop out of their nests each summer into chaos. It works for them. It just seems to me we should do as wood ducks do, and that is not to start jumping out of trees and hoping for the best, but rather to continue doing those things that have worked well for our own species, which is to invent, solve, prepare. Then we'll just have to see how that works out, eh?

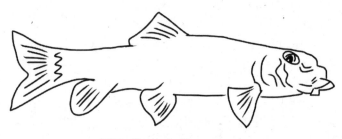

Fit for a Queen

My tackle box has hundreds of spoons, jigs and artificial baits that together cost... well, let's not go there. But walleyes have been neither impressed nor interested in what it has to offer for a couple of weeks now. I decided it was time to go back to a successful philosophy from my childhood, and that was to catch fish, any fish, not just walleyes, and soon enough a smallmouth bass was putting up a good fight at the end of my line. I filleted the bass, figuring a walleye or two on the next night would fill out a meal. It wasn't necessary.

A couple days later, home alone and scanning the fridge for breakfast, I spied the bass fillets and in short order, toast and blueberries were bookends to a plate of sizzling fish topped with a touch of salt and lemon. It was a great breakfast, and I share this knowing there is conflicting opinion on taste in our walleye-crazy northland, where some regard "bass on the table" in a category of "it will keep you alive." But there's more to the story.

Last winter, friends Donny and Mike set up an ice fishing trip for northern pike—a great game fish that again, many consider suitable for little more than pickling. On this day, the big ones apparently took a vacation, leaving mostly two- and three-pound "snakes," as they are called in these parts, to give us battle. Mike made the best of it by filleting up a few of them on the tailgate of his truck. The next thing you know, the drone of a small generator fired up a portable deep fryer, signaling a fish fry was on. It was a meal fit for a queen. It was that good. I'm not kidding. Try it yourself; it will be worth it. You'll tell your friends. Leave the meatloaf sandwich at home.

On yet another day some time ago, my friend and neighbor, Delon, brought me a bottle of canned white suckers he had just made. It had a texture and taste as succulent as salmon. It was so good we ate the fish on crackers until the jar was finished. And suckers are equally as good when smoked. I can tell you one thing and that is if suckers could talk, they would surely want to thank those responsible for naming them "suckers," as this alone likely reduced fishing pressure on them to a level near zero.

It's inevitable in a country of plenty that we have high-scale restaurants that can charge hundreds of dollars for one personalized meal of sushi, which is raw fish rolled with white rice and various vegetables. It must be fantastic fish because white rice is virtually tasteless and vegetables are vegetables. There are also folks with an acute sense of taste who are paid great sums of money to discern fine wines from those less worthy. (Gee, thanks. Now I won't have to go through the painful experience of finding one I like for myself.) These things are fine and good, but they point to the fact that we sometimes create a mystical five-star standard for one thing, which by default diminishes the attributes of another. If the question is: "Does a bass taste as good as a walleye?" it is only right that we should also ask: "Is an apple as good as an orange?" And who said this is a competition, anyway? I don't really care if sausage comes in second to bacon—I'll eat both. And if you happen to like sushi better than sunfish, that's okay. The message in all this is to find out for yourself. Enjoy where the experience takes you, even if it is fishing for suckers.

It would probably take the Queen of England to get some folks to change their opinions on both the taste and sporting value of various fish, because we humans tend to grasp an idea and hold on for dear life. But if we could get the queen to come over for a visit, we could do worse than to serve her a breakfast of Leo's lemon bass fillets, a deep-fried pike lunch provided by Donny and Mike and then Delon's canned sucker surprise on a Ritz with afternoon tea. In the evening, we could take her out fishing for blue gills and end the night with a nice glass of boxed wine served around a campfire. I think the queen would like it all and she'd tell about it and maybe then somebody would finally listen.

I Don't Know

There's an ongoing frenzy over football players and their conduct during the national anthem that some say is un-American. I don't know what to say about that because I haven't "walked a mile in the shoes of" Colin Kaepernick. Colin is the NFL quarterback who started the whole thing last year by kneeling during the national anthem to bring attention to the recent rash of black Americans killed in contacts with law enforcement.

Is he being un-American? I don't know. It's hard to know what it must feel like if your brother was shot reaching for his driver's license or if your parents were not allowed to use "public" bathrooms or your grandmother was arrested for not giving up her seat on the bus for a white man or your great-grandfather was lynched in Duluth for something he didn't do or your great-great-grandmother was a slave who could be whipped or killed "just because." Those kinds of things affect the way a person sees things. And it bothers me to view scenes of white Americans who proudly had their picture taken while fighting black kids who just wanted to go to school or where others were lynched. Chances are that some of those proud folks thought they were patriotic. All these things happened under the same US Constitution we have now.

Is Colin doing the right thing? I don't know and most importantly, I don't know him. He wants systems within our country to improve and he is being peaceful. I can't judge him for that. For me to judge him as un-American is to say in effect that I am a better American than he is. How can I know that, and what is the criteria? Maybe the folks in Wisconsin burning Packers uniforms over this issue are un-American. Is cheating on taxes? Is making billions in profit, then hiding it in another country? Is fraudulently accessing government social programs? How about politicians spending millions on government trips or pharmaceutical companies charging $600 for EpiPens? Is hating other Americans un-American? Is kneeling during the anthem? Which is worse? Somebody, please, number them in order of severity so we can know who is patriotic and who isn't.

I grew up during the Vietnam War, a war that divided our country in almost every way it could, as was so well captured by a PBS special of the same name. Masses protested. Presidents, veterans, clergy and politicians debated whether there should be a war or how it should be fought. Soldiers died, civilians died, billions of dollars were spent. Hidden bombs shattered lives and everywhere there was the rubble and flames of battle. After the war, there was even angry debate over the memorial to honor soldiers who gave their lives in Vietnam. In the end, we were all still Americans who cared about country and other people and we shared in a common grief. If you visit the Vietnam Veterans Memorial (The Wall), you will know what I mean. Maybe I'd have a different opinion on the etiquette of patriotism if I'd had the chance to serve in Vietnam, if I had walked in a soldier's shoes. All I have for reference is two close friends (one who sadly has passed) who did serve there, and each had much different experiences and notions on patriotism and neither was in the business of telling others how to live. The idea that anyone with an opinion can determine who is un-American seems very un-American to me. And it bothers me that someone who may truly be un-American can hide behind a salute to the anthem and criticize others, whether he is a soldier or football player.

We have a country with a constitution that is the most fair, inclusive and protective in the world. Our democracy and our constitution provide opportunities that allow Americans to do great things History shows we (Americans) haven't always been right and we don't always do great things within the framework of a constitution that is indeed great. It is to be expected—we're human.

There are many things I do not know and we can continue to discuss flags and standing and kneeling and anthems and patriotism, but the real issue is, "How can we better protect the public and the police when they interact?" I have police friends and classmates and a young cousin who is training to go into law enforcement. I'm fond of these people and the public too. Don't take me wrong, standing in respect for our anthem and flag and country is an honor and a right, but what is right is not that simple. A quote from the aforementioned documentary on Vietnam maybe said it best: "Patriotism is a complicated matter." There is also a quote that says, "Love your neighbor." We could work on that, too, while we're at it.

Three Kinds of Wise

I don't know about you, but I collect all the advice I can muster on decisions that face me. Even when considering the purchase of something as small as a radio, I compare prices, models and features and I want to know what friends, neighbors and the folks at work have to say about it. Besides making for easy conversation (most folks like giving advice), this approach seems wise, even though it can have the look of indecision. Two heads are better than one, right?

There was one time my exhaustive research and advice-seeking was most fruitful. It came when the idea of buying a boat was introduced to my wife, and it was apparent that the idea was not mutually appreciated. After a year of stopping at every boat dealership we passed in order to "just take a quick look," she finally said in exasperation, "Good grief, just buy a boat! Let's get this over with!" With affirmation like that, I was compelled to buy or face the consequences.

But decisions and doing the right thing or the best thing is usually tougher than buying a boat—like building a cabin, for example. The plan for the cabin we were about to build was to keep a low profile, so it seemed reasonable to make the crawl space as short as possible, maybe just two blocks high, I figured. My buddy and professional contractor, Don Aune, said my idea was unusual. He said a taller crawl space allows easier access. He said we could add height to the crawlspace, then build up the ground around it to still keep a low profile. Then he said, "It's your cabin, so do whatever you want." So, given my expertise in electricity and his as a professional builder, I decided to build the crawl space only two blocks high. It was a mistake. Today, the crawl space is one only an Marine could appreciate and though it was too late, an important lesson was learned: listen to the expert, even if he complains about the lousy fishing spots you bring him to.

To properly cover the idea of wise advice takes more than an article, so we'll need to pass on some "choice cuts of meat," so to speak, and get to one last point. Beyond the wisdom of collective thinking or the wisdom of true experts there is a wisdom that is all too often forgotten, and that is the wisdom of experience, which speaks loudly to our senior citizens. It's a fact not lost on native peoples, who respect the wisdom of years more than many other cultures, at least from what I have seen.

Intelligence, facts and knowledge are gifts indeed, but wisdom speaks as much to an art form as science. It has a presence. It is a sense that fills the white space between facts on a page that can at times deceive. Unlike the spectacle of a churning rapids, wisdom is a deep, slow-moving stream quietly coursing through the forest, minding its own business. Wisdom knows there is usually more than one side to a story. It recognizes that you can't believe everything you hear and if you live by the sword you will die by the sword and that honey catches more flies than vinegar. Wisdom does not fall for "fake news." And who can better prepare for a thousand-mile trip through a vast wilderness than someone who has done it before? Much too often today we take off into variations of "wilderness" without seeking that information. Does that make a person confident, adventurous or just plain foolish? The experience of years brings heart to the brain party, and wouldn't most of us do some things differently if we had the chance to do it over again?

I stake no claim of possessing the wisdom I've seen in the generations before me, but I'm wiser today than when I was eighteen. It takes more to anger me, it takes more to surprise me and it takes less to make me happy, because I've come to know that the most basic things in life are the good things— not new boats (even though that new boat had me purring like a kitten for a while there). You can almost feel wisdom if you take the time. When we don't feel it, that is, if we don't seek out and understand someone who has seen the course already, we run the risk of blundering about in the dark, and that's a bad deal, especially when we're not even aware we're in the dark. Experience matters.

I appreciate sage proverbs and coined wisdoms because they stand the test of time. One saying I heard recently goes, "The way you do anything is the way you do everything." I think it's an interesting thought and I'm not sure if I want to know what light that shines on me. Is it a wise comment? I don't know. What do you think?

Get Out and Fail

Actor Jeremy Renner is best known for his starring role in Hurt Locker (2008), a movie that earned him a nomination for an Academy Award for Best Actor. I happen to know him for what he said in an interview on a morning talk show not long ago, when he stated, "Everything I've accomplished I owe to my father." And the reason he gave was that his father had always encouraged him to "get out there and fail." He told Jeremy to try things, take things head-on and generally, to not let fear of failure set the tone for his life.

As it turned out, Jeremy didn't win the award, but he's okay with that. In fact, he almost wasn't even an actor because he was studying computer science and criminology in college for his career choices until, on a whim, he decided to take an acting class as an elective. The rest is history. Apparently, Jeremy took his father's advice to heart.

It struck me, though, that parents (many parents, anyway), focus on just the opposite for their children: success. We expose young ones, as we should, to books, sports, a spiritual life, other kids, music, fishing, scouting, summer camps, family reunions and all kinds of things to help them grow. We hope they will have a fulfilling career, find the love of their life and develop talents that are uniquely theirs. Most importantly, we want them to be happy. That's a lot of pressure for a parent and a child, but I believe it's the way we are hard-wired. So, to encourage a person to go out into the world and not worry about failure seems to fly in the face of reasoning. Doesn't it?

Maybe the two ideals, preparing for success or preparing for failure, are one and the same since the endgame is happiness, or at least it should be. I think Jeremy's father is on to something though. Failure is common, at least as common as success, and the better we cope with it the better off we are. Any entrepreneur worth his or her salt must be prepared for failure with an exit strategy, otherwise their plan is flawed. Winning or status are not assured to anyone, so what could be better than to learn to be socially adjusted, patient, confident and humble—tools necessary for times we fall short of a goal. If you've ever been in a room with someone who has won at everything, won't accept second place and wants recognition, you were probably looking for the exit.

There are many examples of people who went on despite earlier failures. Abraham Lincoln was defeated in a run for state legislature, failed in business, his sweetheart and young son died, he survived a nervous breakdown, he was defeated for nomination to Congress, lost a re-nomination, was defeated for the Senate, defeated for nomination for vice president, defeated again for Senate and only after all that, he became one of our most important presidents. Albert Einstein could not talk intelligibly until he was nine years old and was later expelled from school. Instead of falling into despair he conjured up the greatest scientific theories the world has ever known. Helen Keller overcame a childhood illness that left her deaf and blind to become a renowned author and advocate for women and labor rights.

The point is that these folks faced setbacks but carried on. Most of us will never achieve such notoriety, but the principle is the same. We each have a purpose. Each can contribute. Each is important. And nobody said it was going to be easy. Get out there and do something and if you happen to fail, so be it. It's called experience. Does advice get any better than that?

Carry on, graduates.

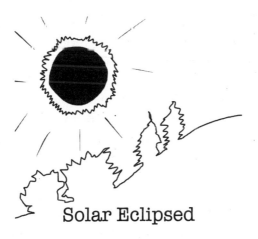

Solar Eclipsed

Bonk, Yak and Bob stepped out of the jungle and gazed across a great valley searching for a juicy mastodon for breakfast. They were chasing mastodons because their gardens had yet again done poorly—cornflakes not being an option. Immediately they noticed the fireball in the sky was dim. It was their first experience with a solar eclipse. Bonk, the leader, said, "Fireball not happy. We go back and eat bugs for breakfast today."

Around the clan campfire that night, Bob, just a teenager, said, "I'm getting tired of eating bugs and chasing mastodons for breakfast. I've been thinking about the fireball lately, and next year I'm going to plant my garden out in the valley so the fireball can show on it. I think vegetables will do better there." Bonk looked at him and said, "Bad idea. We plant garden in jungle because that's where plants live." (This conclusion made some sense, even though they always had a miserable garden.) Then the entire clan began making fun of Bob while throwing sharp sticks at his head, which was their way of dealing with stupid ideas.

Years later, Bob had become an even more inquisitive man who noticed things around him and how one thing could affect another. He also had become a man of great stature, standing six-foot-five, dwarfing his comrades. One day, he thought, I'm going to plant a garden out in the valley this year and if anyone makes fun of me now, I will break their throwing sticks. With this step, the first scientist emerged, and while it marked progress for mankind, it would be slow progress since only very large, intelligent cavemen and cavewomen dared think out of the box for centuries. Not only that, they spent a lot of their time playing basketball.

Thousands of years later, I attended a regional conference for utility communicators offering courses on current events and technological advances in the industry. I jumped at one session that featured an "expert" from Washington, DC, presenting on solar energy, electric cars and battery technology. It wasn't what I expected.

The speaker began by declaring electric cars were a foolish notion that "pander to movie stars and the rich." His odd comment was akin to someone from the rubber industry arguing against rubber tires. But he was the expert, so I listened on. Next, he questioned battery technology that could possibly, sometime in the future, be extremely expensive. Huh? Then he asked, "What do we do with old batteries?" I didn't know. He was the expert. Not so surprisingly, he finished his expensive presentation by noting solar energy and solar charging stations were parts of a pitifully small power network not worth developing. The only thing missing to complete his presentation (other than facts) was smoke coming out of his ears.

I'm not prehistoric but I've been around long enough to "get out of Dodge" once in a while, so I know Bonk-like thinking when I hear it. The presenter was not prepared and offered his opinion as poor substitute to knowledge. If he had been prepared, he may have reported that in 1897, your New York City taxi cab was likely electric, or that the electric Porsche Spyder is the second-fastest production car in the world, or that forty years ago solar electric fences contained cattle and solar battery chargers helped start old tractors (as on our farm), or that a surface area one tenth the size of Nevada has enough potential solar energy to provide the US with all its energy needs. He could have also mentioned that the sun is an incredible mass of energy akin to a ball of lightning made possible by nuclear fusion, the combining of atoms, and that science is working to duplicate this to provide nearly unlimited energy with no radiation byproduct, which nuclear fission, splitting atoms, currently leaves us with. And if we harness fusion, a pail of water could provide as much energy as a supertanker filled with oil. It seems these things would have been interesting.

Now that the world is focused on a rare solar eclipse, it's good to keep in mind that the Sun and energy it provides pose fantastic potential for our planet in addition to its everyday job of making life itself possible. It should be exciting, not threatening, to think that we can someday gain and learn even more from it. Of course, solar technologies and batteries and electric cars need more time to develop before they replace existing technologies, but even Harley-Davidson has a new electric bike they expect will make them the world leader in motorcycle production. That's a big statement from one of the most recognized gas motor–makers in the world.

There will always be voices that, for whatever reason, want to "block the sun," so don't believe everything you hear. The good news is there's lots of room in the valley. Some will continue to plant in the shade, but that leaves more space for a garden out there waiting for you—in the light. I'm with Bob.

Memory, or Lack Thereof

There are a multitude of books, studies, games, exercises and opinions on what a person can do to improve or maintain memory. I get it: memory is important and it's critical to learning and wisdom and depth and love.

My memory happens to be pretty good, or pretty bad, depending how you want to measure it. I can find a spot in the forest years after having been there last, but I can forget where my car is in the Target Center parking ramp. I remember history and literature lessons quite well, but I'm a pour spellar. I recall the setting sun and the very rock we sat on as I proposed to my wife at Peterson's Landing along the shore of Lake Vermilion, then a few years later I forgot our wedding anniversary. On the other hand, my wife has never forgotten our anniversary or my birthday, but she remembers nothing of the night I asked her to marry, let alone the rock. (Maybe I'm not as romantic as I thought.) Anyway, one nice thing about my random memory is that I can read a book again a few years after having read it for the first time. This little twist saves money, which is a good thing.

There is another side of memory, the side that won't forget. It's a problem for people and it's a problem for nations. A while back I watched an interview of two young mothers, one from Israel, the other from Palestine. Each in turn spoke of their love of family, their dreams and their daily routines as their young children played together in the background. They were so similar. Then the interviewer asked how their two peoples may someday be able to live in harmony. Once the topic of peace was introduced, each brandished her remarkable memory of centuries-old sins by her counterpart's nation much like a Samurai warrior may brandish his sword. Not surprisingly, their peoples continue to clash.

I'm just going to take a guess on this, since I'm no expert in peace negotiations as it applies to nations, but it seems some forgetfulness is necessary once in a while. I say this because you can't even bring peace between two three-year-olds if you continue to hash over who dropped the Tootsie Pop in the sand pile and why they did it. Instead, you need to forget about the Tootsie Pop and start anew—done deal. I realize there is more to the story when it comes to nations, but the basics for peace are hard to argue. I guess I'm fortunate my parents didn't harbor resentments to any particular group, or if they did they sure didn't talk about it. From what I could tell, getting along was a high priority and I think they would be happy to be remembered as Americans rather than conservative or progressive, rural, middle class, Lutheran children of Finnish/Swedish immigrants who enjoyed picnics, lest someone take issue with any of those traits. If nothing else, the latter is just too much to remember.

Growing up in the country with few kids around, a poor memory (or the ability to forget, anyway) was like skin—you needed it, especially if you hoped to play a baseball game every now and then. If a kid named Stalin or Genghis Kahn could pitch or even if he couldn't pitch, he'd be as welcome as the next kid. (You can never have too many pitchers, ya know.) And if the second baseman dropped your Tootsie Pop in the sand, you just forgot about it because you need infielders too. That's probably why kids have so much fun – poor memories.

Niskanen, Hannu and Tom

We sat at a streetside table along a harbor in Helsinki waiting for our pizza. It was our first trip "across the water" to meet up with relatives and take in a bit of Finland and Sweden, the lands of my ancestors. People from all walks of life strolled by as trolleys, buses, bikes and cars worked their way through the din. It was a scene familiar to any number of cities in Scandinavia and Europe with its mixture of tradition and diversity. We had barely sat down when a young man in professional attire took the table next to us and, once realizing we were Americans, began a conversation in English, which was a good thing since my Finnish vocabulary includes little more than the words for "what" and "yes."

His name was Tom and unlike the more stoic natives, he was quite talkative. He had moved from Washington, DC, to Finland seventeen years prior to begin a business and said he had to learn the language quickly, noting "there are no shortcuts." (This meant I would not try to use my "Finnglish" greeting "Howsta youla?") Then he brought up the topic of hockey and the fortunes of his favorite team, his hometown NHL champion Washington Capitals. He worried the Caps may not keep their coach and he said his favorite player was an American, Matt Niskanen, their star defensemen. He told us that Niskanen was from a town called Virginia in the state of Minnesota. When I got the chance to respond, I related that I used to work in Virginia, Minnesota, with Matt's father, Chuck. It's a small world indeed.

I didn't know what to expect for the trip. Could we negotiate language barriers? Would we find long-lost relatives? What was almost constant daylight like? What we found were two countries that seem from all appearances "comfortable in their skin," as they say, which in practice made us comfortable. Growth and change is everywhere, as proven by construction cranes, new housing and commercial projects and ever-expanding mass transit systems. The quality of life rating for both countries is in the top ten in the world. Immigrants, even American immigrants, learn the language (don't ask me how) and find a niche among a predominantly blond and white population. Crime rates are low and the police presence was almost invisible in over a week of touring Stockholm and Helsinki. Really. It seems there is a sense of national direction, a respect that stitches peoples together. The evening news is rather bland, with the exception of the political spectacle of the US. People walk, bike and ski more since there are dedicated trails virtually everywhere (both in the city and countryside) to do so. Finland has no traditional energy resources other than wood fiber and relatively poor wind and solar resources, so they religiously conserve, recycle, compost and use only the most efficient technologies. They have universal health care and free post–high school education, both of which are highly popular. All men partake in compulsory military service, similar to our National Guard. Women are currently being considered for the same. Their taxes are higher, which adds a buck to your McSandwich and sets gas at $5.50 per gallon, and these taxes are included upfront in the price of anything you buy. More than one vendor felt it necessary to explain their tax system that supports the infrastructure noted above. I was impressed.

And despite some differences, Finland has much in common with the United States. It is a young republic that survived a bitter civil war and celebrates its independence every year. The rocky landscapes and extreme seasons are similar to northern Minnesota, with the capital of Helsinki looking like downtown Crane Lake on steroids. Finns, like many northlanders, love saunas, their lake or country cottages and time immersed in nature. They even have a male president who is seventy with a young son.

Arriving back home, we were welcomed by the smell of the north woods after a rain, the beauty of a setting sun and a full appreciation of proximity to friends, neighbors and relatives. It reminds me that the Fourth of July, in which we celebrate our country's independence, is indeed more than firecrackers and meat on the grill. Building a country was and is a lot of hard work. But still, if I could be king for a day, I would send Congress for a vacation to Finland and Sweden and for that matter, we could throw in Norway and Denmark—models in new energy technology application. Maybe they would see how other countries both parallel and differ from ours. We in the US argue greatly over many things that other countries don't, or at least, don't have to anymore. Maybe there are things to be learned. And maybe not. When Lewis and Clark began their famous and daring expedition to explore westward, they thought they might come across mammoths and maybe even dinosaurs given the fossil record at the time. That sounds ridiculous now, but when you simply don't know what's out there—you don't know.

Whatever the case, it was great getting together with my welcoming cousin Hannu and his wife, Riitta, and it was a surprise to talk about Matt Niskanen with an enthusiastic African American immigrant to Finland named Tom. And I didn't bother bringing up the 1980 Olympics with anyone—a year when our upstart USA hockey team, featuring a coach and a bunch of kids, like Matt, from Minnesota, beat the heavily favored Finns and Swedes and top-rated USSR to win the gold medal. That and the 1987 Twins championship run were the most significant and memorable sporting events of my entire life. It was great to be an American (and Minnesotan) then and it is still—even if we tend to worry about dinosaurs more than we should.

First Grouse

My young son David and I walked slowly down a forest lane, the ground damp with the rich, musty aroma of decaying leaves in the cool autumn air. It was his first grouse hunt, years ago, and we had not gone far when a bird materialized ahead on the trail. Dave aimed carefully and upon pulling the trigger, an explosion of grass and dirt peppered the grouse, which stood its ground, clueless to the fact that it had been inches from death. No doubt, this was the first hunt for the grouse as well. "Quick, reload, Dave! Take another shot!" I whispered in rushed excitement. Then, with a look of wonder, Dave turned to me and said in a hush, "Boy, those partridges sure are brave!"

On another first grouse hunt, my daughter Beth walked alongside me, again on a forest trail, when we busted a couple of birds out from under a small balsam. One of them rose up into a tree alongside of us as Beth brought up the shotgun and pulled the trigger. Again, the grouse was ruffled a bit but doing just fine in the tree as I looked over to see Beth was a mess. She hadn't held onto the gun correctly and the recoil gave her a bloody nose, fat lip and a face full of tears. I figured she'd want to give it up so I asked if we should just go home, but defiant to my offer, she'd have none of that. This "fight" wasn't over.

Then a few years later, I walked the edge of a tree plantation along Sturgeon River with our youngest, Patrick. He absolutely loved hunting and as a toddler he would anxiously wait at the door for me to come home to tell of the day's hunt and he'd ask as I opened the door, "Did you get one, Dad?" or, "Get a big one, Dad?" As we crested a small hill, three grouse popped up directly in front of us and landed in the nearby pines. I handed the shotgun to Patrick, but in an excited voice he said, "No, you do it!" I replied, "Pat, this is your chance for a bird –here, take the gun!" "I don't want to. I might miss!" Pat whispered back frantically as he shoved the shotgun away. After still more back and forth exchange, which was apparently mesmerizing to the grouse watching nearby, I finally got Patrick to take the gun from me, convincing him that it's okay to miss. It happens to all of us.

Fortunately, each of the kids got their bird and these instances seem to point out that ruffed grouse have a way about them that caters to young first-time grouse hunters. After all, hanging around for supper is a generous habit for a bird that will end up served as supper. On the other hand, the grouse I see tend to explode from under my feet, offering little or no chance for a shot. To say I'm hungry for a meal of grouse is a hint, not a statement. Got partridge? Anyway, besides a hunger for grouse in gravy, these experiences made me realize me they, in no small way, highlighted the personalities of each child.

David saw the situation for what it was and was fairly calm, even a bit analytical about the whole matter. It's how he rolls even today. For Beth, the thought of leaving the woods was almost an insult after being bloodied by the first shot. There was work to do. She wanted to shoot a partridge and no bloody nose was about to dim her determination and yes, she's determined still. For Patrick, his first grouse was about as important as anything in his life up to that point. His pitched excitement lifted a pleasant little outing to something monumental. It was the same type of energy he brought to sports, relationships and his endeavors throughout his nineteen years. We miss him and his energy very much.

Our three children were unique and each approached life in much different ways, even when they were quite young. This was a gift to our family. Likewise, differences in and between people is a gift to our civil discourse and it needs to be respected if we are to benefit through collective wisdom. Maybe we all need to back off a bit from the anger that shadows the debates of the day and try to understand the other side. It's worth a try.

Don't worry. Be happy. Eat partridge.

CHAPTER 5: ADVENTURES

Merry and Memorable

A Desert Experience

I woke up in the back of the van during a much-needed break from driving. My window was hot to the touch as we passed a small town while descending into a one hundred–mile valley of sand, heat and salt known as the Great Salt Lake Desert. It was years ago, and we were on a family vacation.

Beth, our daughter, was driving, the boys read magazines and my wife, "the navigator," was busy studying our course on the map. It was a peaceful scene. After assessing the map myself while resting in the back seat, I asked, "Shouldn't we have gotten gas in that town back there?" The navigator assured us that we would stop at "a spot" that lay ahead. The spot, we were about to find after an hour drive, was just that—a spot on a map with a name. There were no buildings, no people and no gas. Only the remnants of a driveway approach signified progress of any kind. And we would come upon more spots just like it, with a name and nothing else. I suppose it was my fault for not being aware of these things beforehand, but I'm from Minnesota, a state where naming culverts and putting them on the state highway map has not caught on yet.

Surprised by the lack of facilities anywhere, the tone in the van became somber and the next thing you know, five sets of eyes were trained on the gas gauge. To save fuel, Beth smartly slowed to fifty miles per hour, and still later, down to forty. We calculated our mileage, then debated if we were to stall out, whether we should hitchhike as a family or stay with the van and beg for mercy. We didn't have a phone, and the bottle of water we had started with was long gone.

To save you the suspense, we made it across the desert on fumes and limped into a Sinclair service station on the other side. There we shared our renewed love for civilization with three nice young men from Eveleth, Minnesota who were in the Salt Lake City area for the summer conducting hockey clinics.

It's strange the things that stay with you after surviving a desert experience. Maybe that's why so many folks from the northland like to go to desert locations at this time of the year. There must be a good reason, right? All I can say is that our family will have a soft spot for Sinclair gasoline and Eveleth hockey players for the rest of our lives. We just don't do deserts anymore.

Leo Wilenius

Lions and Timbers and Bears

If you spend time outdoors in the northland, it soon becomes obvious that you're not in Kansas. Besides vast stretches of forests and lakes, Minnesota is host to some very wild life and I have been up close and personal with a lot of it.

To list a few, I've been charged by a coyote, mauled by a mallard, have shared a canoe with an otter, saved the life of a fisher and a great blue heron, stood on a basketball court with a white-tailed deer, caught and released forty-four bats in one hour and tapped a wild moose on the butt. I was also nearly trampled by cows twice and treed by a rooster, but those don't qualify since they were "domesticated" animals. Yeah, right—tell them that.

Obviously, there is more to the story in each of these encounters, but it's the "big boys" we'll discuss here. Again, unlike Kansas, where mountain lions, timber wolves, black bears and grizzlies no longer exist, the woods of northern Minnesota are still a haven. I'll share what I know about that.

Black bears (Ursus americanus): Black bears are hungry most of the time. I've had one outside my tent and one inside my cabin, which is backward from most bear stories you hear. A cabin bear can eat two loaves of bread, a dozen eggs, two pounds of bacon, a chicken, a pound of butter and a bag of candy bars in one sitting. If you're ever building a cabin, like I was, it's advisable to install a door before installing a refrigerator filled with a weekend's worth of food. Or else lock your refrigerator. If you are looking for bears, you'll find good bear patches next to good blueberry patches.

Timber wolves (Canis lupus): Wolves are curious. Once while driving an ATV on a woodland trail, a glance to my right caught four timber wolves standing side by side staring at me. It was also the end of the trail and as the four-wheeler coasted to a stop, all four, as if on cue, started trotting directly toward me. There was not a lot of time to think, as they got close quickly, but what came to mind was, *This can't be happening. I'm very unlucky. I'm so unlucky I'm angry. This might be it.* This all happened over a five-second span and as the foursome closed to forty feet I stood up, yelled and waved my arms. They stopped in their tracks. Without taking my eyes off my furry visitors, I turned the ATV around as they looked on, then drove slowly away, shaken but no worse for wear. A person at the International Wolf Center said that the encounter likely involved curious young adults that had never seen a human before or apparently an ATV. Likely so, since they looked more like they were bringing me the newspaper than stalking me. Still, I'll always wonder how close they would have come before their curiosity was satisfied.

Grizzlies (Ursus arctos horribilus): Grizzlies love to play basketball. North Woods Grizzlies do, anyway. Don't challenge them or you'll get killed.

Mountain lions (Puma concolor, or feline sizus of smallus horsus): Lions are extremely shy of humans. Data suggests they are, for the most part, just passing through Minnesota and they are considered a rarity. However, if "just passing through" happens to be through your backyard, the "rarity" part takes on a whole new meaning to your beagle who loves to chase cats. My brother-in-law took a picture of a large cougar near Little Fork and I've talked with several people who have seen them locally over the last few years—one just recently. Mountain lions prey on deer, elk and moose, which suggests I may want a bigger walking stick.

I guess that's what our wilderness is all about—being wild. Wilder than Kansas, anyway. The great north woods will always be my playground and having big critters in it makes things interesting, at the very least. It may even make a person feel more worthy after having survived another day in the field. Or maybe still, it's simply relative, because I'd rather be in the Superior National Forest with lions and timbers and bears than in my cabin with forty-four bats. Oh my!

A Big If

It has begun. I refer to "fishing fever," a condition that wisps me away to dreams of a boat in a calm, sun-drenched bay where hungry walleyes study the rainbow minnow dancing at the end of my line. The boat creeps slowly along the rocky shore as an eagle perched in a grizzled pine shares my search for a breakfast of fresh fish. Yes, again I'm connected to waters released from icy bondage to the jurisdiction of sun, wind and rain, providing memories of good days past and a promise of good days ahead.

Do you have those dreams too? Sometimes they're so vivid you can almost feel the warm sun on your cheeks and the rough sides of a chunky walleye as you pluck the jig from the corner of its jaw. But then, reality returns and you're surprised to be back in the moment especially when you realize you're in rush hour traffic or sitting across from your date, who's desperately working on an excuse as to why he or she must go home early.

But this spring, rather than concentrating on walleyes, bass and panfish, I've decided to think big, applying more time on the water to muskellunge—the fish that looks like a northern pike, fights like a grizzly and eats things large enough to be concerning to folks who like to swim. I've only caught three of them (by accident) over the last thirty years, but this year should be different, as I intend to learn more about their habits and preferences. I also plan to go for "the big one" because folks tell me the world record could be right here in northern Minnesota, and given the monsters I've watched cruise by while fishing for other species, I suspect they're right. Just think—a world-record muskie. I think I'm feeling a "wisp" coming on.

If I happen to catch the world-record muskellunge this year, I'm going to be upfront and confess right now that I intend to keep it and not only that, I plan to go shamelessly commercial. First, I'd take a picture to record the moment for the eons. I'm hoping the grandkids would be with me, since I suspect a guy could get seriously hurt trying to take a selfie with a muskie that's sixty pounds and sixty inches long. The prints, by the way, would go for probably less than ten dollars each. After that there would be calls to make. Assuming I catch it on Vermilion, I'd order a Bamboozler pizza from the Vermilion Club to celebrate. Then I'd call our neighbors, Chuck and Mary, to come over for pizza and show them the fish. I might even have them take a picture of me and the kids with the pizza because a Bamboozler is almost as impressive as a world-record fish.

And to take full financial advantage of the notoriety, no product or promotion would be overlooked because if I catch the world record, muskie hunters everywhere will want to up their chances to do the same by emulating everything I do, not the least of which is to start out every morning with a bowl of Homestead Mills oatmeal. It's healthy, grown locally and it's the breakfast of world-record holders, don't ya know. And when healthy eating isn't enough, you won't find any better medicine on the planet than those from the friendly folks at Franks Pharmacy, where you can count on great service and purchase my new book, How to Catch World-Record Muskies, but given my record on getting books published, don't count on that part. Speaking of books, I recommend you book your next vacation with one of many fine resorts that range from classy to quaint and are located on one of our pristine northland lakes, each posing the chance at record-breaking fish. And don't you dare tackle a fishing vacation without equipping yourself with tackle (like I still have to buy) from the folks at Berkley, Northland, Rapala and Eagle Claw, to name a few.

Of course, I'd be more than happy to share with you the specific pieces of equipment I buy from these folks, the tackle shop I bought it at, the lake on which it would work best, the resort I would prefer to start out from and even the name of my favorite candy bar, for that matter, but it's going to cost somebody because I have yet to pay for the new laptop I bought to write these articles and laptops don't exactly grow on trees, if you get my drift. However, once I get sponsors covered, I may even talk about my world-record muskie for free. More than likely, anyway.

Let the fishing begin!

Say What?

We were next in line at a McDonald's restaurant in San Francisco's Chinatown. It was a family vacation and our three teenagers preferred the familiarity of McDonald's for lunch over the fresh seafood fare my wife and I had. As we waited, the family in line in front of us (who I'm guessing spoke Punjabi) was attempting to order hamburgers from McServer #1, a kid speaking German, and getting help from McServer #2, a girl standing nearby who spoke Chinese and broken English. Given this, I figured it was time to set up camp for the night and send the kids out for firewood because we didn't think this transaction would be completed within the next few days, let alone the next few minutes.

To my surprise, and after a chorus of languages and gestures, the order of hamburgers came across the counter about as quick as you'd expect McDonald's to deliver. It was both entertaining and impressive to watch as each person in the conversation stayed cool and kept smiling. Still to this day, it's hard for me to understand how four languages converged to communicate so well.

Twenty years later, I again found myself standing at a counter wondering how the next exchange was going to work out, but before we get to that, we need to cover why I was there in the first place. Just three weeks ago, I began witnessing my laptop slowly succumbing to a variety of problems. After a number of calls for service, it was apparent that computer-fixing folks (CFFs) are facing the same fate as the white rhinoceros in that you won't find one anywhere. At least, I didn't. I surmise they (CFFs) have finally succumbed to a technical world that replaces equipment rather than repairing it, making for a frustrating state of affairs for folks of my generation. I suspect I'm not the only one with desk drawers full of old watches, calculators, cameras, recorders and other devices I can't bring myself to throw away because, after all, they could be fixed. And in some cases, they still work fine, but are fatally outdated.

Once I finally conceded that I'd have to buy a new computer, it bothered me to spend so much money with so little time to research them and, okay, here's my admission—I'm a little computer illiterate.com. To prepare as least some, I did a crash course on the internet to become semi-fluent in the language of technology. From this intense thirty-minute training I figured I'd need a solid-state drive with enough data storage to document my entire body of writing since the first grade, with enough left to document every cell in my body. Don't ask me why that much is necessary; I'm just going with the experts on this. Then, of course, I'd want the latest processor, which costs twice as much as its predecessor. And if you're going to put these heavy weights into the equation you would be out of your mind (or at least out of memory) if you didn't include enough random-access memory, or RAM. My first thought is that this is a lot of fuss just to write articles for the Cook News Herald, but alas, a good typewriter is even harder to find than a good CFF. A second thought: the Apollo mission that put men on the moon used computers with the computation power of a modern pocket calculator. I'm not kidding.

So now I was standing across the counter from the computer salesman, prepared and confident I could replicate the "miracle in McChinatown" and complete this conversation without appearing too ancient or ignorant. The salesman politely asked, "What can I do for you this morning?" Confidently, I responded, "I need a computer and I'm thinking something with an i7 processor, maybe 256 gigabytes or so of solid-state storage and 16 gigs of memory." And he said, "Very good choices. Which platform were you considering?" SAY WHAT? I thought to myself while my mind raced to determine what he meant. Then he said again, "Have you thought about what platform you want to use?"

Now I've known for a long time that computer geeks (okay, experts) excel at confusing and humiliating us regular Earthlings when we're caught in the black hole of their computer jargon universe, but I had no idea they were this good. I thought that "laptop" might be a good answer, but a wrong answer is even worse than just standing there looking stupid, so I asked the salesman (and I am rather proud of this), "What platform do you think is best?"

Yup, I may not be computer literate, but I still got "it," if I don't say so myself. I might even qualify for a job at McDonald's.

History of Pontoons

A favorite summer pastime of mine is to zip around the lake in pursuit of good fishing, lunch at a local establishment or an open chair around somebody's campfire. But on a recent sunny morning, instead of jumping into the boat, I knocked the spider webs off the canoe and pushed off for a short trip down the shore.

Within minutes, I slipped past an eagle perched close to the water. Further along, a heron scanned a sand beach for breakfast. Rounding the point, a family of mergansers scrambled from an abandoned beaver lodge, where clear water covered in lily pads and a muddy bottom provided habitat for minnows scattering at my approach. This was an enjoyable fifteen minutes spent, and what's cool is that I could jump back in the canoe tomorrow and have another outing just as fine. You simply experience things differently traveling at five miles per hour rather than zipping around at thirty. Contemplation replaces concentration. Relaxation overcomes results. And you notice things around you large and small.

The trip that morning helped me to understand something that has puzzled me for a long time, and that is the explosion in popularity of pontoon boats. I didn't see the phenomenon coming and I didn't understand it until now. (If I had seen it coming, I would have invested heavily in the outdoor lounge furniture industry.) The reason, I believe, is because pontoon boats are essentially an extension of the canoeing experience, which has been a popular cornerstone of the northland for centuries. They are quiet, comfortable and they practically shout out tranquility. And it is no small item that they are much easier to board than a canoe.

You may be surprised to know that the first modern pontoon boat was conceived and built by a Minnesota farmer named Ambrose Weeres in 1952. The fact that he is a Minnesotan may not be surprising to some, but a farmer? Really? I did not find this surprising actually because I grew up on our family farm near Cook, which gives me something of an inside perspective on the probable thought process of Mr. Weeres. Over the last few days I helped put up hay at the farm and I realized, as surely as Mr. Weeres must have, that a pontoon boat has a lot in common with a hay wagon (stay with me here, since you already took the leap from canoe to pontoon boat). Like a pontoon boat, a hay wagon moves along slowly, offering one time to reflect on little things like leopard frogs, cloud formations and the hum of a good, running tractor. More importantly, when I'm on my hay wagon I'm with the people I care about most because my entire family helps with the task—even the grandkids. It's easy to extrapolate that Ambrose's family helped with hay making, too, and it probably wasn't long before he realized that strapping a couple floats to his hay wagon deck could extend the treasured family time that hay season brought. Not only that, his new "pontoon wagon" could bring them fishing, host a picnic and maybe even find a campfire if it was close by.

I suppose I could have saved us all some time to simply

summarize the modern pontoon boat of today as the experience of a canoe made possible by a hay wagon with the option of a 300-horsepower zip drive, but you'd miss the essence of what makes them popular. That much versatility is impressive enough to make me want to have one, but I don't know how my trusty old boat and wife would take it. And if this account of pontoon boats lacks the depth of research that pontoon boat historians had hoped for, keep in mind that for five consecutive days following the Fourth of July, I was standing on a hay wagon while wishing I was on a pontoon boat. It makes sense to me.

Lake Trek

Lake Vermilion: the final frontier. These are the stories of our cabin, Enterprised. Its three-day mission: to explore strange new hobbies, seek out new lifestyles, boldly staying civilized and indoors where man has not been rained on before.

Captain's log, stardate July 12. 1900 hours, deep in the Frazer Bay sector. On what should be a day of discovery on a beautiful July quadrant, we find ourselves negotiating a meteoric downpour. Waves pound the shoreline, keeping the crew on board without a sauna, swim or picnic in open space for two days. Fishing is out of the question, but don't tell that to the two alien lifeforms clinging on to their hydrocraft in four-foot surf starboard of the docking station. We will monitor as to whether they are desperate fishermen or, in fact, Klingon spies. To warm up, we are considering evasive maneuvers to an orbit around Phoenix, Arizona, where it is currently 108° Fahrenheit, not 54° Fahrenheit as it is here. Really.

We made phone contact with relative lifeforms in the far reaches of Head-o-Lake Bay. They are faring better with our four grandchildren, who are stocked with books, Scrabble and a cribbage board. Their transmission stated the kids are working on a secret machine that will allow them to have fun even when the weather is bad. We want it. Any attempts to reach them by water would be futile, unless of course we were to buy a bigger hydrocraft, but I've chosen to visit that black hole in another time zone.

Captain's log, stardate July 13. 0800 hours, deep in the Frazer Bay sector. The crew is restless, with mutiny just one weather forecast away. First Mate Princess Lindy is in her third day working on a puzzle and could possibly be losing her sense of humor. (How was I to know the phaser was loaded?) Private Zippy, our cat, passes time destroying the sofa, which she does on sunny days as well because she is a cat. We believe there is still a functional sun above the stratosphere otherwise the solar electric fence would have failed by now, leaving Gideon gophers and white-tailed deer free access to our meager attempts at a garden. We have not seen neighbors Chuck and Mary in two days and are considering a search party to see if they have left for the Vulcan highlands without taking us with them. Another neighbor, Scotty, has been unable to beam us anywhere, let alone up. Still, with a new book in hand and a supply of fresh strawberries, we continue on our present setting.

Captain's log, stardate July 14. 1100 hours, deep in the

Frazer Bay sector. Staying the course has seen us through the clouds to the cosmic cleansing of sunshine. The federation has decided against retribution on Canada for the repeated low pressure frontal assaults they have so unmercifully sent across our border, so I have given up my commission of leadership and return to civilian life. To celebrate, we have left cabin Enterprised in our hydrocraft at hyperspeed to boldly go somewhere.

If you came to visit us at the Enterprised and found this log book, please leave a message or make yourself comfy, but keep your mitts off the Zup's polish sausages in the fridge. You can find us on an exploratory expedition to Wolfy Way or Bench Warpers for a burger. If you have any issues, please refer them to Lieutenant Zippy, who is probably hiding under the couch. Hoping your phaser is loaded and your anti doesn't matter. X9—The Captain

Good grief, it's nice to get outside again, isn't it? For a while there I thought I was getting cabin fever.

A Wild Walk

It was a late summer night in the early 1970s when I returned home from an evening out and crawled into bed. From the darkness of the bedroom across the hall, my father said in a hushed voice, "Open your window." It was a strange request, but my father was not one to kid around so I got up, slid open the window and waited. In a moment, a low, haunting howl filled the woods across the field. I had never heard nor seen a wolf before. The moment left a lasting impression.

Today, hearing and spotting wolves in the northland is common. And since that night listening out my window, I've come to know firsthand that you need to be careful what you say if you decide to have a conversation with wolves. I'm actually rather skilled at "wolf talk," if I do say so myself, and you can ask my wife. No, on second thought, don't ask my wife. Well, you could ask my wife but she may just confuse the issue so let's leave my wife out of this and take the time here to explain one "conversation" from a late summer night six years ago.

My wife and I (so much for leaving her out of it) walked and talked along a quiet highway one Sunday night when something brought me to an alert halt. It was the barely audible call of a timber wolf in the distance. Cupping my hands, I answered with a short call of my own and within a few seconds, the wolf replied. We walked on until I paused again and let out a long howl. The wolf answered again, but something was different. "That sounded closer, didn't it?" I asked my wife. "Yes, it did," she agreed. This was getting interesting. Now, I took a deep breath and let out a deep, intense howl, but before the call was even finished, the woods before us, not a hundred yards away, exploded in high-pitched yelps and growling synonymous with a heated battle for survival! It's possible the ruckus was a show of force by the pack or perhaps a release of nervous energy in their anticipation of an encounter. Whatever the case, a pack had closed in on our position and they sounded angry. It's possible my call that was intended to say, "Hi guys! How ya doing?" actually came out as "I'm your rival from the pack next door and sure enjoy tramping on your turf over here!"

My wife's facial expression let me know she wasn't impressed with my wolf "discussion." I didn't think we were in danger, but must admit it felt dangerous. Our only sense of security was a walking stick. Within a few seconds, we could hear branches breaking and the cadence of footsteps. Then we strained to see as dark forms began filtering through the thick poplar growth until suddenly, there was movement in the tall mix of brush and grass in the power line right-of-way alongside of us. With a few steps, a large wolf emerged from the grass onto the highway no more than thirty yards away—mostly black with eyes trained directly upon us. It took stock for a second or two and quickly vanished back into the forest with his pack in tow. Just like that, it was over. Let's just say it was an experience that sure beat watching a rerun of Family Feud on a Sunday night!

I admit my "wolf" may need some work, as does my "loon" and my Spanish, but that doesn't distract from the fact that a simple walk in these parts can be quite memorable. And while this experience provided us with drama, it's nothing compared to an animal encounter our cabin neighbor, Judy Harris, had years ago, when she met a bull moose on our shared narrow gravel road and walked right past it (without incident) as another neighbor witnessed the event from up the road. There are instances of walks by other neighbors that intersected closely with black bears, and just a few weeks ago I walked up on a young raccoon striding down a state highway. Okay, maybe the raccoon encounter hardly rates as dramatic, but it shook the dickens out of the raccoon. Indeed, a walk in the northland is like a line in the movie Forrest Gump, where Forrest's mother tells her son, "Life is like a box of chocolates. You never know what you're gonna get." No doubt.

Deer Act

The dappled remains of a fall snow outlined the trail in the black of morning as I headed to my deer stand. It was a special year because this time I wasn't hunting for a buck, I was hunting for the buck, and it was a dandy.

A wisp of wind on my face confirmed that deer ahead shouldn't smell me, but the crunchy snow announced my approach no matter how careful I was. That was a problem, because my deer stand was close to where I expected my quarry could show up and my biggest fear was to jump a deer in the dark, sending it into a noisy, danger-alerting escape. The feeling was tense. I decided to try a trick I'd read about and began acting like a deer, which is not to be confused with a mule impression, as my rude "friends" would suggest. Rather than a rhythmic march, I elevated onto the pads of my feet, taking a step or two and then a pause, another step and a pause to mimic a deer nonchalantly feeding along. The stand was only ten feet away now when a heavy thud just beyond it got my heartbeat racing. Hurried footsteps leading away made it clear my cover was blown. Now what?

Deer season the year before found me anxiously approaching the very same stand, only it was afternoon. Pre-season scouting discovered a fresh buck scrape (a pawed-out patch of ground bucks make to mark their presence) in a small clearing only forty yards away from the stand. A hoof print over five inches long from tip to dewclaw let me know that the maker of this scrape was a big one. I was watching the ground for more sign when I looked up to see that something on the trail that didn't look right. That "something" was a buck (with uniquely wide antlers) that materialized from the edge of the trail, then angled away off the other side without ever sensing my presence. That would be the only sighting of him the entire season.

I waited the next fall to check for telltale sign that would indicate if the buck survived the severe winter, predators, disease, other hunters or, surviving all that, if he was even back in the area. That's a lot of "ifs." Prior to the season I again scouted for sign and there it was—a large bare-dirt scrape in the same place as the year before. It announced to all deer around, and to me, that this particular buck (in all likelihood) was back and staking out his turf for breeding rights. How cool is that?

So there I stood in the dark listening intently to the fading footsteps that carried away any dreams of shooting the "big one." A walk to another stand would have me sweating like a Swede in a sauna, so I climbed into the stand to wait for sufficient light before seeking another option. As dawn broke, features of the woods began to emerge. A small sound behind me deserved attention so, slowly turning my head to find the squirrel that must be the culprit, I instead made out the head of the buck in the dim light not ten yards alongside, intently gazing forward. I desperately wanted to make a move, but any motion would have sent him flying. Not only that, but not expecting to see a deer, I had rested my rifle peacefully against the rail at my far side. The buck, unable to detect danger after a tense minute, was wise enough to know that the appearance of no threat didn't account for what he heard earlier and he melted nervously out of sight into thick brush.

What? I was angry with myself! I survived a "bump in the night" earlier only to now watch the buck walk away from just a few feet away. Piecing together what happened, it was clear that the deer trick had worked. While my steps to the stand earlier were enough to unnerve the buck, they didn't give me away as a human either. The buck had fled but he did so silently in the dark, rather than blowing loudly like an alarmed deer typically does. Now the big guy had come back to see what was creeping on his turf and I wasn't ready. Nuts! Then suddenly a movement to my left woke me from my self-pity and revealed the buck was circling downwind through cover to use his best sense—his nose—to determine if friend or foe had surprised him earlier. Luckily for me, a narrow shooting lane stretched out ahead of his path. After what seemed an eternity, the buck with a wide rack stood silhouetted at the very end of it. Not long after, my son and I pulled a nice deer out of the woods.

That's the story. In less than an hour, I experienced anticipation, shock, despair, intensity and the thrill of a successful hunt. Deer hunting is often like that… and cold. Success may be the result of a good plan or simply luck—I'll take either, thank you. Just as important, beyond the hunting experience, I wasn't computing or watching TV and eating peanuts, because I'm too often "successful" at those things. Folks who don't hunt or don't approve of hunting may have trouble relating to this story, and that's okay. I don't relate to a lot of things, either, such as line dancing or sailing or sweet pickles—what's the deal with those things, anyway?

With snow on the ground and deer season upon us once again, I anticipate more deer stories, regardless of success, and if I need to act like a deer to get one, I will. Wishing you good hunting, honest deer stories, great campfires or whatever works for you in November.

I Get By

I was twenty years old and looking for my new pair of glasses. Couldn't find them anywhere. Searching the house twice over, I was getting cranky before realizing they were perched on top of my head. So, when I mistook a blue-and-white tube of hand cream for a blue-and-white tube of toothpaste in a dimly lit bathroom forty years later, I didn't panic that maybe I was losing it. It was par for the course, a part of my personality, something that makes me special. But it begs the question, "What was the Neutrogena doing next to the Crest in the first place?" On the bright side, after the brushing, my teeth had never been so soft and supple.

Questioning my actions has been a lifelong self-reflection, it seems. After "losing" my glasses and before brushing my teeth with hand cream, there were other happenings. I threw gas on wet firewood smoldering in our furnace, which instantly removed my eyebrows and laced what was left of my eyelashes together like Velcro. I didn't say anything about it at work the next morning, but the crew figured it out in short order; they thought it was funny. A few years later and a week after a knee operation, the knee felt so good I decided to play tennis and tore cartilage in the other knee, making for two surgeries within a few months. Painful. Thinking I was adept at car dealings, the salesman undercut my "firm offer" on a Ford Escort by a thousand bucks as my wife looked on. Embarrassing. One memorable night not long after turning fifty, a friend, Don Aune, offered to help me put in a roll-out dock. After multiple attempts at ramming the dock into the water with no luck, we realized the front legs of the dock were set too far down and were now bent at a forty-five-degree angle from pounding into the bottom of Lake Vermilion. Then, just a few years ago, I climbed into a deer stand anxious to try out a new range finder only to discover I had my garage door opener instead. Fun.

And I still have the touch. On opening day this year, I loaded the boat with the net, tackle box, gloves, poles, life jacket, coffee and minnows. The plug was in, the gas tank filled and the motor tuned like a fine violin. Pushing off from the dock and zipping my phone safely away in my jacket, I remembered I forgot (proving even a poor memory can be useful) the boat motor key. Quickly hooking up the electric trolling motor to an almost-dead trolling battery (forgot to charge it or pack a paddle) I managed to get back to the dock, fetched the key and returned ready to fish. Boating a couple miles to my secret spot, I shut the boat down, hooked up a minnow and into the water it went. Finally, it was time to fish. Before the minnow hit bottom, it occurred to me my new fishing license was safely back in the glove box of the truck (the same place the key had been), so up came the minnow, down went the motor and back to the truck to get my license. After that, I went fishing but didn't expect much luck given the activities previous. Duh.

And when I'm not questioning things I've done, I find myself questioning mysteries of life. Questions like, why do my two vehicles have gas caps on opposite sides? Why is my phone company the most difficult place in the world to contact by phone? Why do people using Facebook get concerned over privacy? Why can we put a man on the moon but can't develop slow-growing grass?

I've written about mishaps before, when it would probably be better keeping these things to myself. Maybe it's a subconscious hope someone will validate me with, "Hey, that happens to me too!" Whatever, I do some smart things too. I get by. It's still fun. I just don't keep score.

Eleven

As is our tradition, on a recent warm night with a dark moon, my wife and I found ourselves on a blanket in the yard looking up into the stars. The evening news said astronomers predicted it would be a good night for viewing a meteor shower, and how they could know that is far beyond me because most everything "up there" is far beyond me both in scope and comprehension. It's just too big.

Indeed, the universe is the biggest thing there is, bigger even than Texas. (Sorry, Texans—that "Alaska" thing had to be tough enough.) For example, when you look at the Big Dipper constellation, you are actually viewing the light that left the surfaces of the seven stars that comprise it about eighty-one years ago. It doesn't take much mathematics to extrapolate that if you have a machine that can travel at the speed of light, or about 671,000,000 miles per hour (and I doubt you do), it would take you eighty-one years to reach the Big Dipper. If you really like space travel, the North Star, which is forty-six times larger than our sun, is 433 light years away, or if you're just looking for a good picnic spot, the universe offers 156 billion light years of exploration. Now does that induce a sense of wonder for anybody out there or is it just me? Like I said, it's really big.

I don't know if I'm more impressed by the scope of the universe or the folks who understand it so well. Over five centuries ago, seafarers in crude boats navigated oceans larger than they could ever imagine by charting the sky until they eventually came across the "new world," and just as amazingly found their way back home. Not so endowed, I can have trouble finding my way from the back forty to our hunting shack with a compass. Anyway, it still amazes me that scientists today can predict celestial movements such as Halley's Comet and solar eclipses far into the future and they can observe tens of thousands of galaxies from any one spot rather easily with basic telescopic equipment. You and I see about 2,000 stars with the naked eye when we lay on a blanket in the yard looking up. Our nine-planet solar system, when compared to the rest of space, is small, but keep in mind it took the Voyager 1 space probe three years just to go past Saturn while traveling away from us at a speed of eleven miles per second. And as review for my sake, if for no one else's, our solar system is a tiny part of the Milky Way galaxy, which contains billions of stars, which is one among billions of galaxies that make up the universe. I may have learned these facts in Mr. Bennick's eighth grade science class, but like a lot of information that was floated by me back then, it didn't land.

As for my wife and I, the unknowns of the night sky can remain mysterious—just viewing the moon, northern lights, meteors or shooting stars, airplanes and satellites is interesting enough. Not only that, but few things are as calming. And to complete a sky watch, we try to stay out long enough to witness at least one truly brilliant falling star. The newscast said it would be a good night, and as usual, they were right. Within a half hour we saw ten falling stars along with six satellites until finally, a streaking meteor, "number eleven," made a long, bright burn across the sky. It was the one we had hoped for—a small connection of sorts to memories, loved ones and our spiritual side. That may sound whimsical to some, but I'd suggest you don't knock it till you've tried it. The universe is an amazing place. Grab a blanket and see for yourself.

A Trip to Remember

We recently took a trip to New York City with a small band of adventurous Minnesotans and to be truthful, it wasn't on my bucket list. At this time of the year I'd rather be on an adventure chasing big game. But I've been curious about New York, so I went along with a healthy dose of apprehension.

Upon arriving, it wasn't long before our group was immersed in the experience because while New York is big (it ain't called the Big Apple for nothin'), it's not all that big in area. After a short bus ride, we stood among the throngs that result from a population of nearly 9 million residents and 60 million tourists yearly. We took in Grand Central Terminal, Rockefeller Center, St. Patrick's Cathedral and Fifth Avenue in the first day. Over the next few, we'd tour Ellis Island, the East River, Central Park, a Broadway show, museums, the New York Philharmonic Symphony and more. If you're an Olympic-class walker like most in the group I was with, you can actually walk to much of it. But a peculiar thing hit me somewhere along the first day—I was comfortable. Me, a seclusion-loving guy who grew up on a dead-end road felt like part of the fabric. Who'd-a thunk? It's funny how fear is so quickly erased by knowledge. Yes, there were odd street performers and some folks who were down on their luck as you will see in any large city, but for the most part, people moved along just as they do at the Minnesota State Fair, taking in the sights while negotiating through pedestrians. I was under more stress dodging white-tailed deer on the early morning drive to the Duluth Airport than at the center of Times Square.

There was a special takeaway from this trip of many experiences, and that was a tour of the 9/11 Memorial, situated on the former location of the World Trade Center twin towers. I wasn't prepared for this moment and as I sit here writing, I am affected still. The memorial conjured up something deep inside. Television coverage during and since the event has looked at every angle over and over and over, to where I find myself sometimes deflecting it for something else—something happier. But the memorial doesn't waver, and one is brought back once again to that fateful day. The news broadcasts, the interviews, people running from and heroes running to the towers—it's all there. And as I walked silently witnessing the event yet again with the residents and tourists of New York City, I was awash in emotion, as were those of many colors and many languages around me. I touched the fender of a fire truck that had been bashed in half by falling debris and listened to desperate phone messages from loved ones and saw bloodied office papers and twisted metal girders. It was a lot to take in.

After I left the building and edged up to one of the reflecting ponds that bears the names of the victims, I stood along the name of Peggy M. Hurt. I looked up her obituary later and it said she died in the Pentagon portion of 9/11 after serving just two weeks on the job. She was thirty-six years old, bright, vibrant, loved her church and loved to sing. She was one of 2,996 who died that day. They're worth remembering.

There was a quote displayed in the memorial that I did not record, but it said something to the effect: "9/11 is more about the goodness of millions rather than the evil of a few," and perhaps that thought was what comprised the lump in my throat as I left the memorial that day. We may not know why a madman bombs a federal building in Oklahoma or a gunman shoots down hundreds at a Las Vegas concert or why terrorists crash planes into buildings in New York, but good always prevails. That seems to be the story the memorial is telling, or at least it was the one I was hearing. As horrible as loss and grief are, they provide a blessing of sorts when we the living are reminded we still have a heart that cares and a tremendous capacity to love. That's a gift. Hate be damned.

Chasing Game

I spend a lot of time in the outdoors because that's where wildlife hangs out, and wherever humans and wildlife meet, there's usually a good story. Sharing these encounters while sitting around a warm campfire is almost my favorite part of the hunt. Young and old have their say and each is as appreciated as the next. Nothing against cozy kitchens and lush living rooms, but campfires have them beat when it comes to sharing stories of the wild.

Speaking of wildlife stories, I recently had lunch with a good friend and classmate, Al Musech. He told of a time when he and his kid brother Cary were exploring just outside of Cook with the Fultz boys when they were charged by an angry mother black bear. It's his story so I won't tell it, but let's just say when you come across an anxious baby bear in a tree, it's best to leave immediately. Maybe even sooner. His story reminds me that I, too, have experience on the subject of intense encounters with wildlife and since I share on just about every aspect of my life beyond the size of my underwear, we may as well cover those.

I've chased almost every kind of game there is around these parts and crazy as it may sound, game has chased me too. As a boy, I found a baby mallard along the creek at our farm that apparently had gotten separated from its mother. Thinking it orphaned, I caught the distressed fuzzball and figured I'd bring it home to raise. Walking back, I sensed something behind me and turned around only to have a hen mallard in full flight smack me in the chest. I dropped the duck, of course, to the care of its mother who, cursing at me still, escorted it back to the creek. That was pretty scary stuff.

On another occasion I hunted grouse next to an old granite quarry, strolling in waist-high ferns along a small mountain of rock. Ahead, the ferns began stirring in a line that clearly indicated an animal shorter than the ferns was coming directly for me. Just a few paces away, a coyote cleared the ferns, still coming directly toward me, and I shot from the waist as it dropped before me. It was an adolescent not much bigger than a fox and my guess is it must have thought I was one of his kin shuffling through the ferns. Dropping down to check it over found that only one BB pellet had hit its nose, apparently knocking it out. I brought the coyote home and kept it in our kennel for a week until it could walk and think straight, then let it go. It loved hot dogs.

Years later, I was stalking the woods on a deer drive when I came out to an old logging trail and saw my daughter waving and jumping about on her stand at the end of the trail. Not hearing any shots, I acknowledged her enthusiasm and pushed on into the woods toward the river and after going just a short distance, found myself in a forest with a moose. Now, I couldn't see the moose, but it had to be a moose or else somebody was driving a truck through the woods ahead of me, smashing through and over everything it encountered. At first the moose was running away but then the sound got louder and louder—it was coming back. Maybe it had detected another hunter on the drive or was looking for different escape route, but I'll never know because I didn't stick around to find out. I was doing some smashing and crashing of my own to get out of those woods. Later, my daughter recounted that she had been trying to warn me that I was hot on the trail of a bull moose and should be cautious. Here I thought she was just happy.

My most unnerving exploit I've written about before. Searching for dry firewood on a four wheeler in a jack pine cutover, I came across four timber wolves watching me intently from a distance away, causing me to come to a halt. As soon as the wheeler stopped, the four comrades began trotting toward me in a confident manner (for a lack of a better term), closing the distance to just over ten yards when I stood up on the machine waving and shouting. They came to a stop and simply watched as I turned the machine around and left the woods. I am not exaggerating to say for a second or two I thought I was a goner. Had I ever been inclined to pee my pants, that would have been my big moment.

Thinking on these encounters, it was probably incorrect for me to say I've been chased by wildlife since the reality was the duck was just being protective, the coyote was mistaken, the moose was confused and the wolves were probably just curious. And I suppose Al's story of being chased by an angry bear tops all of my stories since he truly was being chased. But I'm here to tell you, that mother mallard was really, really mad and it would have killed me if it had the means. It's just a story that doesn't "sell" very well around a campfire, if you know what I mean.

The Navigator

Our family didn't take spring break vacations to warm places when I was young. Not many folks did back then, at least not in my neighborhood. But we did take some nice vacations. We toured Yellowstone, visited Mackinac Island, fished in Canada, shopped at Wall Drug and viewed Niagara Falls up close. In all those trips I don't recall my father having any trouble getting us to where we were going. Unfortunately, it's a talent he did not pass on to me. My wife, "the navigator," as I affectionately call her, doesn't have it either.

One summer day, the navigator and I were slogging along in three lanes of bumper-to-bumper traffic. She looked up from the map to say, "I think... maybe we... hmmm... we should be on that overpass." Well, we happened to be traveling under it, so technically we were close. Undeterred, we drove along for another five miles, maybe ten—felt like twenty—before finding an off-ramp that would allow us to turn around and make another attempt for the exit to the Minnesota State Fair.

Thinking about it, when we travel it's very much like a bullfight in which the bull (our vehicle) charges at a matador (the exit we need). And like the bull, we often miss our target. But that was before we had travel technology. Things were going to change.

This time we were going to the airport in San Juan, Puerto Rico. Again, we were in heavy traffic, but with the aid of a travel app on our smartphone, the navigator could be sure that the ramp we just drove past was the one we should have been on. That was a quantum leap for us. This progress was confirmed a few years later while on vacation in Florida. Returning from the beach, our phone showed in real time that we had missed our turn and the lights in the distance were from Tampa Bay, not Orlando, where our hotel and kids were. (Just so you know, the kids were adults by this time and knew enough to drive their own rental car as opposed to riding with us.)

Today, I can report that we get around in our travels pretty well. And if for some reason technology fails us, I have my internal compass to get us back at the end of the day and, of course, the navigator.

Fishing Secrets

When the spring fishing season began I had hopes of catching the world-record muskie, or at least the state record, and to be sure, there's plenty of time left in the summer for me to do just that… if I stick to it. But "sticking to it" might pose a problem because while pitching for muskie one picturesque evening, I came to realize something significant: muskie fishing is a lot of work. Now, I'm not exactly shy of a hard day's work, but fishing for me lately has been defined more as relaxation than work and this phenomenon is wearing on my resolve.

If you don't understand why muskie fishing is hard work, you don't understand the gear. When fishing for other species I'm using 1/16th-ounce jigs or a three-inch Rapala or a spinner with a leech. In contrast, for muskie, I'm throwing a stick bait or a spinner bait, either of which is nearly a foot long and seemingly closer to a pound than an ounce. After just twenty casts I'm beginning to breathe hard, by thirty I'm sweating and by fifty I'm nursing blisters. I know it's said the muskie is "a fish of a thousand casts," but at that clip it might take me a few years to land one. When I'm either unable or unwilling to cast anymore, I could try some trolling, but that's no picnic either. Trolling with a yellow Swim Whizz is like pulling a shovel tied crossways at the end of your line. It's all I can do to hold on, my stout fishing rod bending over like a banana. Sooner or later, while trolling with my Swim Whizz, some boating passerby will think I'm hooked up with a big one and yell out, "Need help landing that one?" Then I'll say, "No, it's just a Swim Whizz! But thanks anyway!" Given this workload, a good "day" of muskie fishing for me is measured in minutes, not hours. A thousand casts—yeah, right. But that's not the muskie's fault. It's mine.

Decades ago, I read an article in a fishing magazine that told of the four stages of maturation for avid fisherpersons. The beginner catches fish here and there and generally enjoys the sport until such time he or she becomes a proficient angler who has learned fish patterns and their various influences and is often successful at the end of the day. The proficient angler (if his or her spouse will tolerate it) then mutates into a professional fisherman, or simply a fishing maniac without commercial sponsors who knows the fine points of presentation and gear and is ever-driven to catch still more and bigger fish. After these transitions, the professional maniac finally becomes a seasoned angler who has seen it all, or a lot anyway, and tends to "back off" on fishing success to appreciate the experience. Well, I didn't think that would ever happen to me. I thought I'd be a maniac (with beginner skills) for the rest of my life, but I was wrong, and don't bother asking my wife about that as you know what she'd say already. Yes, I'm seasoned and my favorite fishing tactics nowadays tell the tale. Against my better judgement, I'll share these secrets with you now.

Shade: I prefer fishing the shaded areas of tree-crested shorelines or islands when the weather is hot or the sun is glaring, and it is effective on occasion. If a lake has no shade

I'm not interested. Not so surprisingly, I have no desire to fish the ocean.

Midday: Years ago, I was on the water before the sun rose or after every possible morsel of sunlight was gone at the end of the day. Now, the fish I catch bite between 10:00 a.m. and 8:00 p.m. or go without. It makes shade harder to come by since the sun is high in the sky, but it is what it is.

Protected waters: There is nothing like calm water for fishing. My bait lands where I cast it, boat control is easy and my hairdo stays in place. My small boat porpoising through wind-whipped, three-foot swells in pursuit of fish is little more than a distant memory.

Fishing alone: By this I mean fishing without any other boats close by, and this usually occurs quite naturally if you put into practice all of the aforementioned fishing secrets. You see, these secret tactics are indeed more about my comfort and the fishing experience than they are about world records and full live wells. I give credit to crowds that hold tightly to large schools of actively feeding fish in rough, sweeping waters and boisterously cheer for each other on a catch. That's very social and it sounds like they're having a great time, but it's not where I'm at when I have a fishing pole in my hand, and that's okay.

And as I think about it, if it comes to pass that for some crazy reason I'm unsuccessful in my hunt for the world-record muskie by the end of the summer, it's something I can live with. I really should have started this quest earlier, maybe even last year.

A Fudge Option

Resolutions for a new year are not my strong suit because they're usually forgotten by the following week. So much for dedication to self-improvement. That's what resolutions are all about, aren't they: losing weight, learning Spanish, training to dunk a basketball, learning sign language, completing Grandma's Marathon, reading a James Michener novel? To be honest, it took me several years to read Michener's Alaska and the rest of that stuff—poof. By the way, if you have a few years to spare, Alaska is a great read.

Given my dismal record at resolutions, it would make sense to avoid the topic altogether, but no. Apparently there's something in my DNA that will not let a sleeping dog lie. So, for the new year, I've again decided to make a resolution, and have narrowed down the list to two. I'll share them with you now. And in the event one is a failure, the other will be a priority held to fruition by witness of the twenty-six people who have confessed to reading this column at least on occasion.

The first resolution is to learn how to make fudge. Not just any fudge. It has to be fudge like "Sis" (my sister) used to make. Her fudge was chocolate, of course, a little buttery, smooth but a bit grainy and soft. There may be a better word than "soft," but I don't think so, and unlike M&Ms, her fudge would melt in your mouth and in your hands. Indeed, fresh fudge was something that made our place at the end of the road special and it was the place to be, as far as I was concerned—at least while the fudge was warm.

The other resolution is trickier, and that is to publish a collection of these columns from the last year into a book. And while that may not seem difficult given the writing part is mostly done, it's tricky because getting published is not "easy as fudge," as the saying goes. Years ago, I submitted an article to a magazine and their curt response went, in effect, "Thank you for thinking of us, Leo. It sure has been nice weather lately, hasn't it? We don't want the article you sent us and good luck with whatever. Sincerely, the staff of Dream Crusher Magazine." The experience was a hit to the ego, but sometime later it was heartening to learn the magazine went out of business. Satisfying vengeance aside, times change and now that one can self-publish online, it seems there's a chance. Still, I'd rather submit my work to a book publisher who, unlike Dream Crusher, would respond with, "This is really good work, Leo. We'll provide editing, of course, and take care of distribution and promotion. After that, royalties are 10% on the first one hundred thousand books sold and 5% on sales over a million, of course, if that is okay by you. Would $20,000 and a new Harley-Davidson motorcycle be acceptable compensation as down payment or would you rather have a white Corvette?"

Yup, that sure would be nice, but I called a publisher the other day for a reality check and she said, in effect, "Thank you for contacting us, Leo. It sure has been nice weather lately, hasn't it? Have you checked into self-publishing? Self-publishing is really good. Send us an example of your writing and if by some unexpected stroke of poor judgment we decide to publish your offering, be prepared for a lot of work because you'll need to provide promotion, which requires book signings, speaking engagements, etc." Now I was totally prepared for rejection, but the part about "a lot of work" snapped my jaw like a sharp left hook. The publisher wasn't sympathetic, either, when I told her I was retired and as such was trying to avoid work.

Still, I approach the new year with renewed energy. If a book is successfully published I'll let you know, because like the lady said, promotion is up to me. But if history repeats itself and I don't get published, there are twenty-six lucky readers out there who are in for the best fudge of their lives!

CHAPTER 6: HOME

Community in Minnesota's North Woods

Play Ball

Growing up on a farm on a dead-end road had a unique effect on my youth as a fair amount of time was spent alone with my thoughts. It was a positive experience, but it had issues too. Most notable was that our six closest neighbors lived about a mile away, and their average age was about seventy-five years. Suffice to say, it was hard to put together a baseball team on a summer afternoon.

My sister was nice to have around, of course, but she preferred cerebral activities over playing catch, so I spent plenty of time alone looking under rocks, exploring in the woods and running from cattle. The point of this short introduction is that I didn't see many kids during my youth other than at school, so I worked hard to make friends when a kid eventually did come around. Any kid was fine. It mattered little if they were faster, slower, richer, poorer, smaller, bigger, blacker, browner or whiter—under twenty was a plus. And one way I found to get along with such a variety of kids was to go along. If someone asked me for help with their chores or to go swimming in April or to act as a human target or to play chess or to see if that thing was hot or to play baseball—I was their guy. Most of the time these adventures were fun and some of the time they were... well... growing experiences.

Fast forward five decades to a visit with an old acquaintance, who asked, "Why don't you write now that you're retired?" "Writing" is in reference to writing about something as opposed to writing to somebody. I didn't have an immediate answer, but the notion hung around.

Apparently old habits die hard, and again, "going along" seems worth the risk, or at least, like another growing experience. I will write—about something—a duty I performed as a part of my employment. Not necessarily to make friends, even though that would be nice, but rather to get back into the game, so to speak. I'll use my senses honed as a young boy living on a dead-end road passing time noticing things, exploring and getting along, even when the neighbor "kids" were seventy-five or so and didn't play baseball.

Actually, I think my neighborhood could have put together a decent team. Mr. Vainio would have been a good pitcher since he could toss firewood with anyone, despite being ninety and missing a few fingers from cutting firewood. Mr. Niemi, who was only eighty, would have been a natural catcher since he was pretty close to the ground even when he was standing up. Mr. Lindstrom was a little younger, always drove Fords and looked to be a baller, perhaps a shortstop, but he was such a quiet man I would not have dared to ask.

All I know is he was a nice man, and as far as I'm concerned, that was enough to earn a spot on the team.

Randomly Proceeding

Nelmi Koivu was a beloved contributor to the Cook News Herald for many years, and more than one person has likened this column to hers. That's a compliment, but it's fair to say her mastery of finding the vast and random detail in the lives of so many people is unmatched. And while I'm no Nelmi, I had a connection with her. In high school, Nelmi worked with my father, her classmate, on a school newsletter. I, too, worked on a school newsletter. Nelmi also babysat me on occasion when I was little. Maybe something rubbed off. Whatever, let's get random with some news if for no other reason than it worked for Nelmi.

I get comments from readers and for the most part they're well-intended, including, "I don't care what anybody says, I enjoy your writing," or "I suppose a lot of those things you write about could actually have happened," or "I like all of your stories except for one." (I didn't ask which one and now wish I would have.) My favorite comment was, "Thank you."

I've noticed there are very few crickets these days. Nobody seems to care about that, but maybe it's because nobody has noticed. I enjoy crickets; they provide a mesmerizing summer sound and unlike many of our summer bugs, they don't bite. Crickets, unfortunately, are easy lunch for many critters in the wild such as frogs, toads, snakes and even bats, but since there are very few of those around anymore either, it shouldn't be the problem. If someday you hear crickets are on the endangered list, remember you heard it here first.

I'm a baby boomer, in the midst of those born between 1945 and 1965. I couldn't miss watching Elvis in the movie Blue Hawaii when it played at the Cook Comet Theater in the early '60s. I could do the schottische at wedding dances with my mother. I played the trumpet in the high school band, although my band director said it sounded more like I was playing around with a trumpet. My personal music collection consists of 45 and 33 rpm records, cassettes and 8-track tapes beginning with Johnny Horton, Dion, Bob Dylan, Roberta Flack, Creedence Clearwater Revival, the Beatles and the Carpenters and it came to a halt soon after the Eagles and Fleetwood Mac because our babies kept me too busy to listen to music after that. It seems music and the stories it told of love and social changes were a central and uniting theme for boomers. Maybe we need more music.

Best smell. This spring, I snapped off a small poplar sapling to use as a walking stick as my wife and I strolled along the road. The bark peeled easily, releasing an aroma about as good as you'll ever want to put your nose to—fresh, natural, unique. A bit farther down the drive, we walked past a thicket of blooming thistles with large purple flowers in full splendor. If a peeled poplar tree is not the best smell ever, it comes in second only to a weed: the thistle. The aroma of raspberries rates up there too. Just my expert opinion.

Love the memory of a day in about 1977, while working

on an electric distribution line in Nett Lake. A strong storm came out of nowhere, unleashing a downpour. A half dozen or more kids, including brothers Charlie and Dana, who had befriended me, were watching the progress from nearby and since we were away from shelter I yelled for the boys to get in the truck and out of the rain. Seven of us jammed into a single cab for the next fifteen minutes, akin to sardines in a can, and in short time curious little hands pushed, pulled and turned every button on the dash. In a jumble of questions, they inquisitively asked, "What is this for?" "How does this thing work?" "What happens when I push this?" At the same time, I was barking back, "That's for the emergency lights!" "Don't touch that one! You might break it!" The memory makes me smile still.

While waiting unsuccessfully for Vikings game highlights on ESPN yet again, I suffered through a long, boring commentary by three correspondents on the progress, problems, history, marital statuses, favorite foods, hopes and dreams of the Dallas Cowboys. (It's a small-market reality Vikings fans must endure.) After the first two correspondents had their say, the third, Stephen A. Smith, in his blunt and exaggerated way, said loudly, "Somebody has to tell me why we're talking about the Cowboys in the first place! An underachieving team that has won two playoff games in the last twenty years!" I have nothing against the Cowboys—after all, I used to want to be one—but I will always hold a "special place" for Mr. Smith and his statement. He spoke for small-market fans across the land.

Finally, Gerry Ruuska and Beth Sprouls poured coffee while serving delicious, creamy brownies and pumpkin bars at Trinity Lutheran Church last Sunday following the service. I'm told parishioners are hoping for even more good treats as the month comes to an end and new servers begin their duties in November. These "sources" also said that while more brownies and pumpkin bars are not necessary, they, along with cake with sugar frosting, are much better than anything containing raisins. Ahem.

Welk Effect

The end of March marks a period that tests the perseverance of many folks living in the northland. It has too much of this, not enough of that and the weather has trouble deciding between rain, snow, warm, cold, melting ice or making ice. Put it all together and you have the ingredients for cabin fever.

It's an accepted theory that a happy life is balanced and accounts for basic needs: social, physical, spiritual, emotional, occupational and intellectual. I do my best to work on this balance, especially during cabin fever season, so it was a concern that attending a basketball tournament held in Minneapolis in March might disrupt my focus. In fact, it seemed to help. Following is a report card of sorts on how it went in those critical areas.

Social (interacting with people on a social basis): I grew up on a dead-end road near Cook where solitude was, if not invented, perfected. Over three days at this tournament I visited with kids I coached thirty years ago, former neighbors who came from thousands of miles away, neighbors who live next door, my high school coach, cousins, nephews, nieces, in-laws and people whose names I don't remember. I'm here to tell you, I am socially charged to the point of giving off sparks.

Physical (proper diet, rest and exercise): Our diet (if that is what it must be called) included four food groups: pizza, donuts, chips and hamburgers. My wife, "the exerciser," will not allow us to use a hotel elevator, so we recorded thousands of steps in the stairway between going to games and foraging for pizza places. Next time I'll pack an apple and sleep on the way down to improve in this area.

Spiritual (recognizing a greater power): I said a few prayers during the tournament, but most impressive was witnessing a sixty-footer from half-court at the end of the first game. It's the biggest prayer I've ever seen in person, not to mention that the prayer was answered immediately. I was floating about for a few hours after. Now that's spiritual.

Intellectual (life-long learning): Studying my tournament guide during idle moments, I learned the names, heights, grades and schools of 500-plus basketball players throughout Minnesota. Did you know that LaHenry Gills of Austin is just a tenth grader? Not sure where this can be used, but LaHenry would probably get a kick out of this if he were to read it.

Occupational (fulfilling employment): I'm retired so this didn't apply to me, but I noticed the North Woods coaches have chosen well and seem to like what they're doing. It was inspirational. (The North Woods team did quite well, by the way.)

Emotional (love and support): You can't bottle it, but there was something in the air at the tournament, both on the floor and in the stands. I need to stop here before I get emotional again.

So, it went really well. I returned home Saturday afternoon feeling happy, balanced and cabin-fever free. We unpacked the luggage, filled the squirrel feeder (it's supposed to be a bird feeder) and went for a walk. That evening, I turned on the tube to find the Lawrence Welk Show on. No offense to Lawrence and his thirty years of reruns, but the moment was a reality check that things were back to normal. There would be no pumping fists in the air or visiting old friends or eating late-night pizza or watching prayers come true. The driveway is coated with six inches of slush and there is firewood to cut. It was a thundering close to what had been several very special days.

But really, I'm good. I just need to toughen up a bit because it's still March.

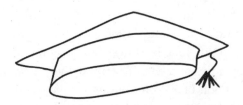

Food for Thought

It's graduation season. A time of celebration, handshakes, tears, pride, hope, potato salad, baked beans, pasta salad, cheesy potatoes, sloppy Joes, wild rice and most important of all: cake. Preferably cake with sugar frosting, and as long as I'm wishing, cake made by Cook's Shirley Hyppa, who is perhaps the best cake maker ever. Excuse me, we got off the subject, didn't we? Let's see—oh yes, graduation.

There is something special about graduation, or more specifically, graduates. There is an aura about them that seems to me a mix of confidence with doubt, pride with humility and happiness with apprehension. It's good stuff. It's so good, something or someone deserves credit for these inspirational people about to enter into the world, because they're not just born that way. Or are they?

Born: DNA, the blueprint of every life, determines much of who we are or may become. We share 99.9% of our genes with all other humans, with just 0.1% of our genes making us truly unique. Physical appearance, strength, intelligence, tendencies for health and tendencies for disease, creativity, propensity for excellence in various disciplines and even personality are, to a point, out of your hands you are born with it. But before we conclude that the DNA "made me do it," keep in mind that 60% of our DNA is nearly identical to that of a fruit fly.

Made: It's what happens after birth that sets us apart from other critters that rely on instinct and it needs to happen in a hurry: learning. Studies show that a baby's brain needs to be nurtured right from the start because by the time the child is four years old, the capacity for learning is nearly set for life. Given this, it is essential that we talk with, read to, play with, snuggle, cuddle, teach, soothe and sing with a little person who doesn't return the favor in equal measure. Of course, there will be crying, arguing and occasional tantrums, but we should expect that from parents since bringing up a little one is stressful at times. Learning allows us to adapt, so even babies quickly recognize the hazards of "hot" or "green beans." We can learn to excel in specific disciplines. We can be laden with hardships, yet still learn to be happy. Even unusual talents of genius need the commitment to learn more, for as the saying goes, "Genius without perseverance is wasted."

Environment: We are also imprinted, which adds a certain flavor to one's personality and values. Because of this, you probably didn't learn to love Chevys on merit. If the parents like nature, reading, hockey, volunteering, folk music and Chevys, there is a good chance their children will share many of the same sentiments. Besides our parents, we're constantly imprinted by siblings and friends, teachers and coaches, pastors and neighbors, coworkers, employers and even unknown people setting examples that stay with us. Point is, your community both immediate and at large is as important as learning and DNA to the final product we call a "graduate." This information isn't new, but it's important, and it's important to remember if you happen to be building a graduate or a community.

To graduates, I wish for you strong horses for times when plowing is tough, fresh bait for times when fishing is good, a community for times you need support and a big heart, just because. And to readers who feel they make the best white cake with sugar frosting, I'd be glad to give you my opinion.

A Good Night Of Ball

On a recent summer eve, two softball pitchers, Addy and Helen, lead the Grizzlies' girls' youth softball team to a victory over Greenway at the Northwood's field. Leaving that game for another, I watched Louie pitch a gem while Micaden cracked a home run to lead the Cook PeeWee's over Cotton in a playoff game. When arriving home later, the news report showed the Minnesota Twins coming from behind to top the Kansas City Royals. Yup, it was a satisfying summer night for local baseball fans and it made me wonder what "Doc" Heiam would have to say about it if he were still with us. Doc, besides being a doctor, was an avid baseball fan who was responsible for the creation of the town's first baseball field.

It was sixty-four years ago this summer that Dr. W.C. Heiam's favorite baseball team, the "Cook A.C.s" won the adult men's baseball league championship that included teams from Tower, Orr, Nett Lake, Aurora, Gilbert, Mt. Iron and Biwabik. And he helped recruit top players for the team namely Clyde Hendy, Chuck Knapp, Andy Grebenc, Lloyd Kantola, Dick Reichel, Harold Baumgartner, Ken Nakari, Darrel Carlson, Elmer Aagard, Dick Whiteside, Kenny Hill and Jack Parr. Doc would also sell tickets to the games while young Doug Johnson (our future state senator) kept score and shagged foul balls as Ray Ronning (originator of Cook Building Center) filled in at umpire when paid umpires weren't available. Merchants in town paid for the uniforms and the players were responsible for maintaining the field. On any given summer Sunday afternoon, the stadium bleachers at the old field (located at the site of the new water tower) were filled with ticket-buying spectators cheering on their hometown A.C.s. It paints a pleasant picture of yesteryear, doesn't it?

Unless you're from the area and over a half century old you probably don't know much about Dr. Heiam if anything at all. He was the first doctor to call our area home - an area that just a few decades prior had been home only to the Ojibwa nation and the first Scandinavian and European immigrants who had carved out homesteads from the forest. And beyond his love for the game of baseball and flower gardens which were kept so neatly by his wife Margaret, Doc had a vision that the

Cook area needed a hospital. A new, well-equipped hospital that could serve and grow with the community far beyond what his small practice located downtown could provide. The concept was big. The need was growing. The vision was right on target. And in 1959, five years after the AC's championship season, the Cook Community Hospital became a reality.

There are a number of things that come to mind from these good ol' days of promoting baseball and hospitals - the sense of community, volunteering, pride and the heritage of these things passed down for the generations to come. Dr. Heiam, from what I gathered about him, was an inspiration because he cared about people and institutions before his own interests. But the theme to his story is not about a hospital or baseball – it's about love. Love is a term oft misused to the point that it can lose its importance. I profess that I love to fish or love pizza when maybe "enjoy" was the appropriate word. Love is much more. It girds the universal truths of right. Love mends, unites and builds. And just like the powerful proper-ty of gravity that ensures the tallest mountains, in time, will weather down to a level plane, so too, did Doc's love prevail to "move mountains."

Today, Dr. Heiam's "power of one" is carried on in mul-tiples. The hospital through the efforts of the community at large continues to grow and each year a "Heiam Ball" cele-brates and supports his vision still almost sixty years later. Unfortunately, there's no longer an adult baseball league and semi-professional baseball never developed in Cook as Doc had hoped. There are however, over a hundred local boys and girls playing ball this summer with uniforms and volun-teer coaches and folks selling hotdogs and helping to main-tain the fields and others building first-class facilities to serve the fields and paid umpires. You don't even need a ticket to watch. I bet Doc would be OK with that.

Autumn Guest

Years ago, a friend and former co-worker, Carol Pohto, had a ruffed grouse encounter which is immortalized here in Autumn Guest.

Autumn Guest

A guest stopped by the other day,
a partridge gilded brown and gray.

How peculiar to have gone astray
and beautify the peaceful yard.

So wondrous was this cautious grouse
while seeking clover along the house,

Without a care—without a spouse—
a fleeting moment to be off-guard.

For even birds need time to rest
from predators or the drive to nest,

To enjoy those things that they like best,
where life is daily sparred.

Back and forth the bird would comb,
a pleasant gift to watch it roam,

It looked to feel as if at home.
Oh, such a peaceful yard.

Then something popped this tranquil bubble,
for suddenly the bird sensed trouble.

It bolted blindly on the double
and hit the window very hard.

How pitiful this feathered wreck
now laying low upon the deck.

She picked it up and wrung its neck
then fried the fowl in crackling lard.

If there's a lesson to be learned,
sometimes life is chance, not earned.

Watch where you're going or you'll get burned,
or fried till lightly charred.

Shopping for Answers

When I summarize the end of my father's life in conversation it goes like this: On Valentine's Day 2007 my father, who was eighty-seven, drove to Cook to do some shopping at Zup's Food Market. That night he passed quietly among family and a team of doctors and while it was sad, his life—how he lived it and how he left it—was a good story. A pretty good "ticket" to buy, if you could, the way I see it.

And while his life was a good one in most ways we judge life, that is not to say it was easy. Life, we must remember, includes trials. His childhood was not exactly happy. He lost both parents when in his early twenties. He mourned for two brothers and two sisters. My mother, his ever-present companion, passed a decade before him, leaving him broken. A year after that, he would lose his best support and friend, Walter, and later still, he would attend the funeral of his grandson. These parts of his story sound painful, but they reflect the kind of experiences many of us will share if we live to be eighty-seven. Fortunately for us, we are surrounded by a lot of good stuff that makes the journey worthwhile.

After his passing, it was necessary to see that bills were paid, accounts closed and forms prepared to retire the estate. Going through his checkbook one day to search for unfinished business, it became apparent that Dad was a regular customer of Zup's. By regular I mean really regular—daily. And while he may have missed a day here and there, a thirty-mile round trip to shop at Zup's was regular routine over his last couple years. It shouldn't have been a surprise. He was often gone when I'd drop in for coffee and his sizable basement pantry, the chest freezer, a hallway pantry and the refrigerator were always stocked as if Thanksgiving Day dinner for fifty was about to be hosted. *But why,* I asked myself, *did he think he needed so much food?*

The answer eventually dawned on me and it wasn't that Dad needed to shop daily for food; his appetite was small to begin with. Instead, what he got from Zup's Food Market was something much more: human connections. Of course, he had the support of family and friends, but it's quiet living alone at the end of a dead-end road and his need to be in touch with the greater human race pushed him through good weather and bad to share in just a few small pleasantries. I suspect it would go like this:

"So how are the roads today, Mr. Wilenius?"

"Not bad. When are you going to get in more salted fish?"

"We're getting more next Tuesday. You know, you were one of my brother's favorite teachers."

"I don't remember your brother, but that's nice."

"Well, have a good day, Mr. Wilenius, and remember— fish next Tuesday!"

"Thank you, I'll be here."

Such insignificant conversation and occasional meeting with familiar folks in the aisles satisfied an important social need for my father. I've told Matt Zupancich of Zup's about this story before, because my father's interactions with the employees there was some of that good stuff mentioned earlier that makes sad stuff tolerable. I have much gratitude for Matt and the employees of Zup's Food Market for being there for my father, and for my family, for that matter. Their team is a great "neighbor," creating many good stories for people in the area, and it takes more than a fire in their store to overcome that.

Leo Wilenius

Four Reasons

A while back, a local newspaper posed an interesting writing assignment, "Why the northland will always be my home." It hit me as a wake-up call with the message that we should consider our blessings every now and then, lest we complain our lives away. Given this, it's an exercise in appreciation that's worth repeating and I'm going to do that here. So, to the point "Why the northland will always be my home," I've listed my four reasons. There may actually be as many as seven or eight reasons but I'm sticking to the basics. The reasons the northland will always be my home are:

Dave's Pizza. It's been my good fortune to eat pizza across the US and my favorite is still a Dave's in Virginia. And if it wasn't a Dave's, there is good argument that best pizza would be from Sammy's or Rudi's in Hibbing, Bimbo's in Side Lake, Poor Gary's on Vermilion, the Viking Bar in Bear River, the Crescent or South Switch near Cook, Choppy's or Snicker's in Chisholm or Sir G's in Ely and I could name others. Indeed, the northland may be famous for taconite, golf, Beargrease winner Jamie Nelson and the BWCA, but for me it's pizza Valhalla.

Roots. A sense of place is special. I was born in Chisholm, raised near Cook and employed in Virginia and Mountain Iron. On a visit to any town in the area, I'll bump into people I've worked with, competed with, been on a committee with, or simply have seen randomly over the years. I don't always know their names, but I know them, if you know what I mean. A move south to Cherry, west to Grand Rapids or east to Ely would still have me alongside good neighbors and within close proximity to a good pizza place. Not only that, if I were to leave the northland, my wife would kill me, but that doesn't count for one of my reasons.

Lakes. What else needs to be said? With thousands of miles of pristine shoreline and millions of fish, sooner or later, I could catch a world-record. Wouldn't want to miss that. Did you know that there's a half dozen places on Lake Vermilion alone that serve pizza?

Care and support. It's said, "It takes a village to raise a child," not to mention a small fortune and some sleepless nights. But the point is that there are many caring people around here who have supported me and my family over the years. Teachers, coaches, churches, communities, friends and people who hardly even know us have been there for us in so many ways I can't begin to name them. It's humbling and it's the stuff that makes for a happy life. And of course, there's the pizza thing.

Other than wishing pizzas were low in cholesterol, I'm happy as a clam here in the northland and I'm staying put. It's home.

Sunday Afternoon

It's Sunday afternoon as this is written and the power is off, out, nada. I don't know about you, but when the power goes out, I'm hit with the urge to run to the refrigerator. I don't know if it's a basic instinct that keeps me from starving to death or simply a phobia of needing to watch ice cream bars melt while I hold the refrigerator door open. Where's the pickles? I need ice. Goodness gracious—the meat! Who will save the meat? If I were to remain calm and consider a peanut butter sandwich for a snack to save me from the ravages of malnutrition, the refrigerator would do quite fine keeping food cold for many hours. All it asks is to be left alone. And, oh yeah, the ice cream bars. Who will save the ice cream bars?

This summer, if you haven't noticed, has been wrought by short periods of high winds, torrential rain, soft rain, rain in the middle, hail and lightning. My garden is not quite pulverized to a pulp, but don't try to tell my beets that. I sense mosquitoes massing at the border of my neighbor's place, waiting for a calm night to attack my evening campfire. With plenty of nice days aside, these multiple storms are enough to make even an anthill want to give it up for the season.

Fact is, I spent my entire career working locally in the power industry, and whether I was at work or now retired, I have heard the cries of the people. Some cries are louder than others, but in the end, most folks really want their power back on quickly, despite the fact that a fallen 200-year-old pine tree in the yard has the power line looking like a bad backlash on my level-wind fishing reel. But I get it. I want power as well. Just an hour or two without it reminds me how much I like electricity. So here I am on a muggy Sunday afternoon with a battery-powered laptop, writing when I'd rather be watching a rerun of The Outlaw Josey Wales for the tenth time or listening to the Twins. Good grief, how long will this suffering last?

After a few years of retirement, I still feel the urge to help when the power goes out, but I've come to appreciate a fact I've known for decades—there is nobody who wants my power to be back on more than the power company. And rather than concentrating all of my attention on why someone there did not cut down the giant pine tree in anticipation of its demise, I'm learning to relax a bit more. Now I am writing, but after that I'll grill and after that I'll take a long walk— the same things I'd be doing if the power was on. And I'll say a little prayer for the folks at the power company because many of them have hardly had the chance to grill or go for a walk this summer. Most sadly, they have hardly had the time to grieve since one of their own, a young man named Drew, passed away while working in a tangled right of way trying to put the power back on after the last storm. Drew was a caring and hard-working person, which is as fine a eulogy as anyone can hope for, and he was the right person for the job. He will be missed. It's a difficult thing for a family and a small town.

After my walk, if the power is not on, I'll start up my small generator to run my refrigerator. If for some reason the generator doesn't start, I will do my part as the hardy North-lander I profess to be by resisting the temptation to stand at the refrigerator door to monitor the ice cream bars in the freezer. Or maybe I'll just eat them. It's the least I can do.

Mileage Matters

Folks in our neck of the woods are used to driving long distances to do what needs to be done—school, work, shopping, etc.—and folks in Crane Lake are a good example. Not to be pitied, Crane Lakers have it pretty good, living close to fine dining, great fishing, boating, hunting, camping and a golf course, no less. That's about as good as it gets as far as I'm concerned, but still, one cannot live on fish and ten over par alone, so they drive. Given this, mileage and the price of gas are legitimate concerns.

It was about 1980 and a few of us were talking about gas mileage in the employee break room when our company engineer shared a story from a family reunion. At his reunion, the topic of mileage came up with a relative who worked in the logging industry, and he learned that his 1976 three-quarter-ton pickup truck was getting about the same mileage as a loaded eighteen-wheeled logging truck, about nine miles per gallon. At the time I was driving a 1971 "boat on wheels," otherwise known as a full-size family car, that got twelve miles per gallon. Let's just say the era was better known for inspired music than for inspired engineering.

But that was then and this is now. Pickup trucks today routinely earn mileage in the twenties, and some manufacturers have several car models rated forty miles per gallon or better. It's progress that really should be celebrated. When the infamous oil embargo hit in 1973, gas prices in the US nearly doubled overnight after decades of cheap, stable fuel. I recall suffering sticker shock at the Standard station in Cook when learning gas had risen from $0.33 per gallon to $0.52 per gallon. The price of gas would continue to climb faster than most other commodities as Americans learned for the first time that energy could not be taken lightly, especially if your truck was getting nine miles per gallon and you lived in Crane Lake.

As a result of the oil embargo, Congress mandated domestic car makers to increase the fuel efficiency of their fleet; politicians had recognized a problem and proposed a solution. US auto makers and the engineering community responded with vehicles that met the challenge, while consumers and the industry benefited through lower expenses. It didn't happen overnight, but it happened and it was a good moment in our history.

But sometimes poor gas mileage is necessary, especially if you want to go fast. One loud example of this is a Top Fuel dragster, which inhales five gallons of nitro-methane fuel as it zips to 330 miles per hour in under four seconds in the quarter mile. That is the same fuel consumption rate as a fully loaded 747 jumbo jet, but with four times the energy. It's enough energy to take an efficient car from Crane Lake to Green Bay to pick up cheese for the hunting shack and your Vikings jersey from the Green Bay dry cleaners.

It might surprise you to know that the dragster makes an

F-22 fighter jet look like a mileage champ, since this jet can cruise at a fuel-sipping five miles per gallon. But let's face it, if you're flying an F-22 fighter jet from Green Bay to get back to Crane Lake for opening day of deer season, you want to get there fast, so let's kick in the afterburners for a time-saving, 1,500 miles per hour that consumes fuel at thirty-three gallons per mile. Remember to sight in your rifle when you get off the plane.

For extreme speed freaks, though, there is nothing like a good ol' Saturn V rocket, which is famous for carrying Apollo missions to the moon. Climbing two hundred miles to reach orbit, the Saturn V is little more than a million-gallon gas tank propelled by rocket engines burning a mixture of liquid oxygen, liquid hydrogen and kerosene at a rate of 9,000 gallons per mile! The speed of the rocket as it climbs is similar to that of a commercial plane (about 600 miles per hour), but what is truly impressive is the fact that once in space, the Saturn's third set of rockets give an extra push, sending the orbiter coasting at 17,000 miles per hour (your deer rifle bullet travels 2,000 miles per hour) for the rest of the trip without the need for any fuel at all. Now that's economy folks in Crane Lake can appreciate! Leaves change in the pocket for the deer license, bullets, blaze orange and boat gas, ya know.

"Just a Gift"

We started building a lake cabin in 1987, which is easy to remember because it was also the first championship year for the Minnesota Twins. As we worked, we listened to them on the radio as Puckett, Viola, Gaetti, Gladden, Blyleven and of course, Cook resident, Rick Appleby's stunt double, Kent Hrbek, took turns as hero on alternate nights on their march to an amazing World Series title over Saint Louis. Homer Hankies, the deafening crowd in the Metrodome and family baseball games in the backyard featuring our kids—Beth Lombardozzi, Davey Puckett and Patrick Brunansky—made for fantastic memories. Sorry, but it seems we were talking about building a cabin before drifting away on the Twins, so let's get back to it.

Three years later and having spent every loose nickel on materials, the cabin was taking shape. One day, I was working alone at the cabin on a sheetrock wall, because it's best I work alone when wrestling with sheetrock. While cleaning tools in the backyard, our lake neighbors' son-in-law from California, Rocky Gomez, came striding down the driveway with a package in hand. It would be quite a surprise.

It was just a couple weeks earlier that my wife and I were discussing décor for the cabin. We thought a piece of artwork with a maritime theme, perhaps a sailboat, would be nice. Yes, we'd shop for one as soon as we could. It was motivating to talk about decorating after years of working with cement, lumber and nails.

So Rocky walked up and said, "I have a little something for your cabin." He pulled out a beautiful watercolor of a sailboat at harbor in a matted frame that was exactly what we had been thinking about. I laughed and said, "Thank you, Rocky! Lindy must have said something, huh?" Rocky looked puzzled and answered back, "Who said what?" Figuring she must have commissioned the work, I said again, "My wife must have mentioned we were looking for something just like this." He said, "I don't know what you're talking about. It's just a gift for helping my in-laws." (Earlier that year I had fixed some things at their cabin.)

As it turned out, Rocky was a professional painter and his subject was primarily sailboats and harbor scenes. We didn't know that. And Rocky had no idea that we were looking for a piece of artwork, let alone one with sailboats. And most certainly, I had not done enough fixing to deserve such a fine piece of art in return. The coincidence and kindness were both memorable and poignant because a short time later Rocky passed away. The picture holds so much more significance for us now.

This little story may not sound significant, yet the coincidence strikes us as amazing still. It seems there was a lot of "amazing" going around back in those days, because it wasn't long before the Twins would win a second World Series title. Thinking about Rocky, his painting that still adorns the center of our cabin and the antics of those colorful Minnesota Twins bring back good memories. I suppose that's the definition of a gift that keeps on giving, and that deserves another "thank you."

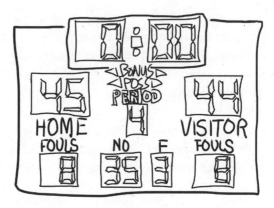

The Score

The scoreboard showed a few seconds left in the game, Mountain Iron High: 45–Cook High: 44. Cook had already lost their first game of the season to Babbitt by two points, followed by a frustrating one-point loss to Ely. Now they, or perhaps I should say "we" (I was one of the players) were looking at the likelihood of yet another close loss on a cold night in 1973.

We had the ball, so Coach Roy Hokkanen called a time-out to set up one last play. It was a basic scheme to rotate the ball to our best shooter, Randy Pearson, with a post player under the bucket to pull in the defense. So here we go. Tim Harkonen threw the ball in to Darrel Brodeen, who passed it to me. Mountain Iron was also aware that Randy was our best option so they had him guarded like Fort Knox. There was no choice for me other than to take the ball to the hoop, where Tom Soderberg managed to find an opening. He got the pass, he scored, Cook won.

Anyone who has played basketball for any length of time can tell a similar story. Many games are won or lost in the last seconds. Why this particular scene from long ago stands out is because the plan was to have Randy score, but instead, he was the only one on this play who did not touch the ball. Tom, on the other hand, was not expected to touch the ball, yet he scored to win. In other words, nothing went according to plan but we won anyway.

But that's basketball. Sometimes things don't work out like you expect. Ask number-one seeds Duke and Villanova, who now watch the NCAA basketball tournament from the stands. By the way, if coaches seem a bit quirky every so often, now you know why. Fortunately for the North Woods Grizzlies boys basketball team, things worked out exactly as they should have this year the best team in the northland won the regional tournament.

It is in times like these that one can fill buckets with the number of well-deserved accolades being shared with the team, coaches and supporting cast. The good will is uplifting. Given this, it's unfortunate that we as a community so seldom communicate or, God forbid, share our feelings, with our youth. So, let's fix that right here and now. And to be clear, winning is nice but it's not everything.

To the Grizzlies: Yes, we are proud of you, but more importantly, we are happy for you. You're nice guys. We know a fair amount about you and we talk about you with our friends and neighbors. You have more fans than you know. Even Great-Grandma, who had never been to a game before, knows you play at a high level. Your skill and effort show loudly.

And while we're at it, we want the girl Grizzlies and those in other sports to know that we see your tremendous efforts as well. Maybe these efforts have been an infectious part of the reason students of North Woods work so hard in so many things such as in band, choir, youth sports, spelling bees, theatrical performances, academics, scouting, those "Empty Bowl" makers, BOSS volunteers, advocates and others who we fail to mention here.

We appreciate what you do to represent the school while bringing communities together in the effort. You are each a treasured part of the northland and we, well, we like you very much. When was the last time somebody told you that? Just sayin'.

Living Simply

I'm like a lot of folks in the northland who would prefer a simple life with maybe a little place in the country, a sharp axe, a boat, a sturdy pair of snowshoes, a grill, a tractor, a snowmobile, satellite TV, health insurance and a vacation home in Florida. That's it. And a cell phone.

Indeed, the idea of living simply is different for everyone and it has changed from the days of my grandparents, who carved homesteads out of the wilderness of rural Cook around 1900. For them, simply living required a source of water, some cattle and chickens, tools for cutting, building and planting, and one nice outfit for Sunday gatherings. Picnics, dances, sports and music comprised their recreation and all told, that was a good life.

But there's another side to living simply and it is told by a fellow named David Owen, who describes his first seven years of marriage like this: "Our living space measured just seven hundred square feet (twenty-five by twenty-eight as example) and we didn't have a lawn, a clothes dryer or a car. We did our grocery shopping on foot and when we needed to travel longer distances we used public transportation. Because space at home was scarce, we seldom acquired new possessions of significant size." One could deduce that David Owen lived in a little cabin nearby here, but in fact, he is the author of Green Metropolis and he speaks of living in an apartment in Manhattan, a borough of New York City.

It might surprise or maybe even anger you when Owen suggests the 8,600,000 people of New York City live simpler, more efficient and "greener" lives than, let's say, the 200,000 robust, nature-loving, independent and good-looking Northlanders in St. Louis County. But the facts are clear, and lucky for us there are places like New York City. For one, NYC is easier on our environment because it is easier on water, woods and wildlife, using only 300 square miles of land, compared to St. Louis County, which spreads its small population over 7,000 square miles. If the people living there suddenly decided they would like to be here to share our lifestyle, our population density of 32 people per square mile would rise to 1,400 per square mile. This shared love of nature, in effect, would make for one continuous metropolis from Duluth to Crane Lake and from Ely to Nett Lake and while it would certainly increase burger sales around here, it would virtually eliminate most of what we love about this place, with the exception of mosquitoes.

But regarding efficiency, there is no comparison. Yes, New York City has high costs, but in terms of energy and many activities, city dwellers are efficient. As Mr. Owens notes, living spaces are smaller, daily essentials are within walking distance and car ownership is optional. And they own less stuff because for most folks, snow blowers, lawn mowers and tractors are unnecessary. And that efficiency helps everyone, not just city folk. One example: A bridge leading to my childhood home on a dead-end road was replaced a few years ago, and I am here to tell you that I and the seven other property owners beyond that bridge should be glad someone else is helping us pay for it. I'm not sure what a new bridge costs nowadays, but it is likely more than we can afford by selling bakery items at the Bear River Fair. The same example applies in the costs to provide roads, utilities, schools and the domestic goods we buy. I personally drive thirty miles round trip for milk, gas, church and banking. Any food provided by fishing, our small garden or the five grouse harvested this fall doesn't exactly qualify us as living off the land. In the end, numbers matter. A large, concentrated population can build things like libraries and concert halls and still help me pay for my bridge.

All this said, I like it here in the northland and wouldn't have it any other way. We are blessed indeed but having a little gratitude toward places like our Twin Cities, New York City and Los Angeles is fair. But we don't want those big city folks to get inflated over this so let's just keep it to ourselves, eh?

CHAPTER 7: LIVING

Progress and Predicaments

Leo Wilenius

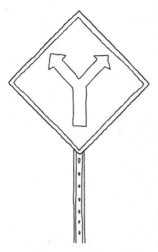

A Lesson from Mr. Choquette

Vernon Choquette was a Cook High School English teacher with the build of a brick wall and a gaze just as imposing. It's fair to say he looked to be a man who would crush rocks with his bare hands for entertainment. In fact, Mr. Choquette was a thoughtful man and as inspiring of a teacher as the school ever had—and it had many.

One book discussion he had with our class was on the premise that life is a random path with "Y"s in the road. And no matter how much we think we're in control, we simply can't predict all the outcomes of our choices at these crossroads, large or small. That's deep material for a kid usually more interested in a girl across the room. Here's an example of his "Y principle":

Sue, a college English major, accepts an invitation to her roommate's home in Singapore over spring break. She loves the culture and agrees to write some ads for her hosts' growing family business. They hire her full time and three years later she's the marketing director for the largest potato chip factory in Singapore. We go back to the invitation again, only this time Sue declines and stays home to study. At the library she meets a student from Iowa who tells her about job openings back home. Three years later she is married, with child, teaching English and coaching softball at Ames Junior High. Two very different life paths developed from one yes or no question—the proverbial "Y" in the road.

After graduating from high school, I was undecided about careers. A short list included forestry, teaching English or history and several electric-related trades. All I needed to do was work out the pros and cons. Well, that didn't happen and as the start of the school year approached, my father, who was efficient with words, did not quiz or coach me, but instead, said firmly, "You need to make a decision." So, with consideration rivaling that of a flip of a coin, I made a decision and got started on the first of many "Y"s in my life.

If I could do it over, there would certainly be more preparation for some of those choices, but it's also good to remember that we are not completely self-made men and women. Sometimes we're lucky. Lucky for having good teachers and mentors, lucky that we guessed well at a crossroads or lucky for being born in the US. Rarely do we or can we appreciate just how fortunate we are as we go through life.

The caption under my graduation picture speaks to that time. Inspired by Mr. Choquette and delivered in real life by my father, it reads, "I don't know where I'm going, but I'm on my way." I adopted the mantra as my own and today, it may do little more than get me off the couch. What will happen then is yet to be determined, but if I've learned anything, it's that action usually beats good intentions.

This story doesn't need a moral to come to a close, but if it were to have one, I think Mr. Choquette would prefer: "Decide, get going, repeat. Fortune-tellers are overrated."

Tackle Problems Now

It's easy to understand why many folks procrastinate when it comes to solving difficult problems. For one thing, there may be no easy answers. But from my experience, putting off solutions only allows problems to grow. So, a few days ago when it was sixty degrees and sunny, I did what always needs doing in spring, and brought out the tackle box for cleaning and inventory. And as usual, there were problems.

First, it was apparent the box had been tipped over or else the grandkids had been using it as a football. Whatever the case, hundreds of items with hooks, hair, line, leaders, bodies and blades had become one mass that could be picked up with just two fingers. I couldn't help but notice the coincidence, or maybe the guy was a fisherman, but Einstein's theory of relativity, $E=mc^2$, summed it up well: energy (the amount of work required) equals mass (all the hooks in a tackle box stuck together) times the speed of light squared (the number of minutes it would take to separate them).

Next, pulling back the trays exposed what my nose had warned about. A leaky fish scent bottle created a slurry of sinkers, swivels, beads and Band-Aids on the bottom of the box. Cleaning up this mess was akin to changing diapers, without the benefit of a cute baby to talk with.

It would be nice if on occasion the tackle box would surprise me with something pleasant, like, "Look! Here's that

$100 bill you were looking for!" but no. It's often a mess and sometimes a slurry, but hey, it's good times—fishing season is at hand! But the job isn't done. Now that the basement is clean and lures are set neatly in their places, it is obvious that inventory is low. My wife didn't think it looked low, but a trained eye can see that we'll need jigs in several colors, some shallow-diving crankbaits, beads, hooks and a couple muskie lures, for a start.

Purchasing tackle is both fun and terrifying, especially if you have kids you need to put through college. Tackle shops are spectacular places with tens of thousands of colorful items you need, could use, would like to try, don't need at all and have never seen before. Most are small and each has a price tag, which means an ordinary grocery bag can hold hundreds, even thousands of dollars in tackle. It's a problem that haunts me every year and it makes me think like Einstein. Why not tackle the problem (please excuse the tortured use of words) scientifically using skills learned from John Geiselman, my high school physics teacher?

The idea is that since I spend a small fortune on fishing, I could own a tackle shop and make good money selling to myself. This is based on the theory of perpetual motion, wherein once energy sets something moving, it can be manipulated to go on in a continuous loop—a nice idea, but it doesn't account for resistance due to friction. My surprisingly simple formula accounts for this and reads: $ET=(SxD)-R$, or in longhand, enough tackle equals shopping (in hours) times dollars (available), minus resistance (send spouse to Little Fork to visit her sister). It needs work but fishing season is close so I'll need to start experimenting—maybe next week.

Getting Started

It's said if you are going to write, you should write about things you know. Well, I know something about a lot of things, not much about some things and quite a bit about other things. Unfortunately, the things I know quite a bit about do not generate income anymore, or at least that's what the Cook News editor, Gary Albertson, is telling me.

But given the large list of things I know at least something about, it's often hard for me to get started because I am decision-challenged and always have been. At age six, I couldn't decide if I should go to first grade or just stay home and learn how to read first. My early teens would find both bell-bottom jeans and cowboy boots in my closet. After high school I nearly had to flip a coin to decide on more schooling or career path. Today, the simple question of hamburger or cheeseburger is difficult enough, not to mention onions or not and chips or fries. Then of course there is an almost endless choice of what to drink. Gee whiz, all I want is a nice meal at the South Switch. Can't somebody just bring me something?

So rather than writing about anything in particular, it seemed worthwhile to share some of the themes being considered for future pieces. Following is a categorized, but not complete list of ideas I've been putting together over time for this writing adventure. Some may or may not reach print, but that's the nature of inspiration—it's a crapshoot. Hmm, that sounds deep. Well, anyway, here's a list.

Hard Starting: Old snowmobiles I have owned, next year's firewood, creating my own country, cleaning my room, playing basketball at six in the morning, motivating volunteer roof shinglers and piano movers.

Undesirable Animal Mixes: White clothing and black labs or black clothing and white labs, a motorcycle and deer using the same highway, mosquitoes and campfires, blueberries and stinkbugs, a sand fly behind your glasses, meatloaf and dogs in the same kitchen, squirrel feeder or bird feeder.

Bad Ideas: A ten-year-old with a whoopee cushion, dusting the house with a leaf blower, Todd Swanson's Burmese tiger trap, tubes of toothpaste and hand cream in the same drawer, studying chemical reactions at age five, swimming in Bloodsucker Bend, cleaning "clutter" from my wife's closet (yeah, that's bad), the improper use of tools, testing electric fences the old-fashioned way.

Good Stuff: Maple nut ice cream, one dock and two grandkids and nine bass, a sandy beach in March, pizza, physical therapy, watching stars from a boat, comfortable shoes.

Frustrating Fifties: Fifty degrees in February and fifty degrees in July, fifty shades of black remote controls, turning fifty, fifty ways to peeve your lover (inspired by Paul Simon), the downside of fifty-fifty, fifty-year-old hay balers.

People: People I know and people I don't know. (Donny Aune owes me twenty bucks.)

Deep Things: Relating inspiration to a crapshoot.

Shhh! The Baby's Awake.

Cute as a bug and she was all ours.

Dating was fun. Getting married was exciting. Learning to live with another person in good times and bad was a grand adventure, but a baby? Now that's spectacular stuff! I don't need to explain how special it is, whether you've had a baby of your own or you've been a part of a baby's life as a family member or friend. Even the cat and dog know it's special.

The first time I held Beth, she must have sensed something big was happening, so she showed off for her nervous first-time dad with a hiccup, a burp and a yawn as I did my best to hold on and not break anything. Is it not out of balance that we need training and a license to drive a motorcycle but nothing to raise a baby? After the birth and just a day or two in the hospital, a nurse walks you to the exit and says, "Beautiful baby you have there. See ya!" With a new motorcycle you at least get an owner's manual. (I rest my case.)

After about a year and a half, it became apparent that we didn't have just any ol' cute baby on our hands. She was smart, and more than anything, inquisitive beyond belief (nice talk for destructive). Anything in the house that was three feet from the floor or lower she would rearrange, pull apart, break or flush down the toilet. A natural at multitasking, she could turn expensive stereo needles and stereo albums into household trash in mere seconds. Doilies, decorations or anything on an end table—she'd have none of it. Dog food was first come, first served. The cat was on high alert. To say that our house was "baby proof" by the time she was two just doesn't tell the story. From floor to counter top, the house was essentially empty.

With this, we eventually learned that when the baby was awake, we would often do what we could to keep her from getting involved in projects we were working on. It was a tag-team event. I'd whisper something like, "Honey, I'm going to clean my tackle box out on the deck," to which my wife would whisper back, "Okay, just watch her close out there, because I've got to clean up the kitchen." Or my wife would say, "I'm going to work on my quilt project, so would you keep her busy?" And I'd say, "I'm changing oil in the truck. How about I just put her in the high chair with a few record albums till I'm done?" I embellish a bit, but that was more or less how it went.

One sunny fall Saturday served as inspiration for a hike to scout for new deer stand sites. Beth and I were home alone for the day, which didn't look to be an obstacle. After all, what could she break in the woods? After finding the baby back-pack in the garage we (baby, me, the dog and lots of snacks) were in the truck and on our way. Easy peasy. Once reaching the old homestead that we planned to walk, it became apparent that our little yellow backpack was fine for a seven-pound infant but not so much for our twenty-pound toddler. Somehow, we got her squeezed into the backpack and set onto the tailgate of the truck. Then it was my turn to squeeze into the straps that were designed for a 120-pound person, not a 190-pound one. If you've ever watched a puppy chase its tail, you know how that went.

After getting the pack on I got my footing, grabbed the snacks, found the dog and down the trail we went, just a talkin' away. "That's a bush. Pretty bug. Yes. We can't eat that! Biiiig tree. Another pretty bug! Yes, mommy's coming home soon." You know, a typical hiking discussion. When we left the trail to meander in the thick woods, the reality of an undersized backpack became apparent. Twenty pounds in a properly sized backpack is no problem. However, put twenty pounds centered near your neck and suddenly a walk through a thick forest becomes nearly impossible. You're top-heavy, Scooter.

After a couple stumbles, it was obvious this adventure was a bad idea—we'd had enough. Arriving back at the truck, we discovered unloading was not as simple as reversing the loading process. Finding a grassy place, I got down on my knees and began to pry myself out of the backpack, until the precious load and momentum took on a life of its own. We fell the last short distance to the ground in a heap. Beth was startled, but fine, I was fine, but startled, the dog was eating spilled snacks and the backpack was retired all in an instant.

It was a clumsy moment that was embarrassing even though there was nobody there to witness it. After coaxing a smile from her, I knew all was well on this sunny hillside in the grass and it was time to go. It was her first hiking trip. This summer, Beth, along with her mother, aunt and cousins hiked across the Grand Canyon. Apparently, she's still inquisitive and doesn't mind a good hike. I'm taking just a little credit for getting her started at an early age.

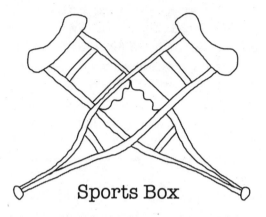

Sports Box

I like to play basketball a couple mornings a week, compliments of the Community Education program at North Woods School. I'm here to tell you that it's not easy, and that's a sentiment shared by other players my vintage. First you have to consider we play against guys who are only in their forties and fifties, and some are even younger than that. But competition is competition and it's still fun after all these years—just a little painful.

So, a couple weeks ago while complaining about aches and pains from the first morning of ball, one of the guys mentioned he relies heavily on his collection of joint supports. It reminded me that I, too, have some of those goods, and given a nagging ankle pain from last basketball season, I went home to see what the inventory had to offer. It was easy to find because my stuff is all neatly arranged in a wall of labeled totes in the basement: "Fall Boots," "Hats," "Gloves," "Sweaters," "Photographs," etc. A quick look and there it was—the "Sports" box.

Going through the Sports box was a reality check. First, it brought back memories of more active days in the form of a batting glove, biking shorts, a mouthguard, jump rope, a baseball and a few other such things. Then, it became obvious what taking part in sports over the decades has evolved to—a laced ankle brace, two elastic ankle braces, four types of knee braces, two exercise bands for shoulder therapy, a tennis elbow wrap, a bowling wrist support, four more variations of wrist braces, three arch supports, a small elastic bandage wrap and a large elastic bandage wrap. The only thing missing for a fully-stocked triage center was an IV stand, a few units of blood and crutches. But the transformation of the Sports box didn't happen overnight.

About twenty-five years ago, as I groaned on the couch after a couple hours of Alango basketball league action, my wife commented, "Maybe it's time you give it up." I responded, "I'll go till I'm forty." Well, that mark was missed by a couple decades of what I call "good hurt" and part of my motivation is, "If Arlee Olson can do it, why can't I?" (Arlee was near sixty and would show up at the Alango gym now and then to play.) I'm not sure what motivates other experienced guys like Rick Aune or Randy Swenson to continue to play, but they must have something, because waking up at five in the morning to chase "jackrabbits in sneakers" takes more than a hot breakfast.

Anyway, I took out the ankle brace, the big white one with laces, and it felt good—less pain. A few days later, my yearly checkup at the Cook Hospital found that my pulse is excellent, my blood pressure is good and my ankle is broken. As you can imagine, I was as surprised as anyone to find out that my blood pressure was good!

Doctor Holmes went on to say I need to wear the ankle brace continuously for four to eight weeks and I shouldn't do anything strenuous, which means no more three-mile walks with my wife. He also said it was a bad idea to climb trees to work on deer stands. Not walking I can deal with, but the stand thing is a problem. Deer season is just around the corner and I'm not done preparing. There are stands to fix and shooting lanes to cut.

For more than four decades my Sports box has taken me through some tough times, but it's apparent that it can't provide me with the one thing I need for the situation I'm in now: more time to heal. I saw it coming. Maybe if you don't have a broken ankle and don't have anything planned for next weekend, we could get together for lunch. I'll buy. After that, I'd be glad to show you some of my deer stands.

For the Record

At a company meeting a number of years ago, a newly hired manager said he wanted to establish a mindset where all could excel in their individual efforts toward a high-functioning "team." The goals: professional growth, personal happiness and to create the best company we could. He went on to say that just once he'd been part of such a team and it continued to be a positive force in his life, and he wanted that for us too. I didn't bother to raise my hand to say I had already done that—it would have been awkward. But I knew exactly what he was talking about.

In the fall of 1973, the Cook High football team, under the guidance of Coach Roy Hokkanen, began a season that was hopeful for a playoff year, and by the end of the regular season the team was undefeated. So far so good, right? But as fate would have it, football playoffs at that time were based on a computer points rating system, and a scheduling issue left the Gophers with one fewer game than other teams. The top four teams in the state went to the playoffs—Cook finished the season ranked fifth.

I was fortunate to be a part of that team and that new manager was right. It's great to know the feeling of being part of a high-performing, well-oiled machine. Still, the experience of coming so close to a state playoff berth was a frustration that bothered me for years. Maybe it still does forty-four years later (talk about holding a grudge). I'd like to share a little about that.

Coach Hokkanen had a simple philosophy that everything important to a play in football needed to happen within the first second of the snap of the ball. He wanted an explosion, not just execution, whether on offense or defense. Field position and defense were treasured over first downs and the theory certainly worked, since the team did not give up a touchdown until the fifth game of the season, and of course that was to Orr. Our best measure of success was defeating a talented and unbeaten team from Cherry in the final game of the year 34–14.

For the record, as fullback, I needed only to follow our center, Marty Walker, through the holes that he and his line mates routinely provided. As defensive back, I played the same side of the field as end Darrell Sandberg, who was a force. Put simply, this job was even easier than fullback, since Darrell would crush any pass or run attempt to our side of the field before I could get there. Truth be told, I could have read comic books and drank Kool-Aid during the game and we would have still done well. On defense, I had more in common with the cheerleaders than the other players, that is, "Nice hit, Darrell! Good job, Darrell!" More accolades could be said of all members of the team, but you get the idea. There—I feel better now.

The 2017 version of the North Woods Grizzlies football team was most deserving to make it to state. They were a machine in their execution that toppled an extremely strong field of competition and they often made it look easy. I suppose that's one of the things a high-performance spirit brings to the table, whether in sports, in school, in a family or your work, where each person is dedicated to a goal, prepared and willing to work hard—the job gets easier. That's a good thing to remember and it is a gift these Grizzlies will keep for a lifetime.

Soon I will be eating a terrific turkey and super stuffing prepared by my wife, along with Beth's great green bean casserole, Peggy's perfect vegetables, Gail's wonderful wild rice, Mary's marvelous fruit salad and Auntie Irene's best-ever banana crème pie while sharing inspirational conversation with family and friends. Apparently, the pursuit of excellence is catchy. And I'm here to tell you that once you've had high-performance mashed potatoes and gravy, you don't want to go back!

Practically Christmas

Our electric clothes dryer started making noise last month and next thing you know it had a broken belt. I'm guessing it was a bad bearing but you know how that goes—it can cost more to fix them than they're worth. And it seems such a waste, since we bought the dryer in 1980 from our neighbors Miller and Gert, which means it couldn't have been any more than forty to forty-five years old. I hope our chest freezer, which is about the same age, hangs in there because Christmas is coming and we can ill afford any more frivolous spending. And I sure wasn't about to pass the dryer off as my wife's Christmas present. (Wasn't born yesterday, ya know.)

Speaking of Christmas, I've been thinking about gifts lately, and after this many years it's hard to know what to ask for. I'm wondering if electric shavers today are better than the ones I have. Yes, I have two. One is a plug-in electric one my folks bought me in high school and the "new" one is a cordless model I bought a couple decades later. But if I were to get a new razor, I'd have three of them, and that seems wasteful if not indulgent. I don't exactly have a forest of facial hair, so maybe I'll see if the old ones can be sharpened.

A new sound system would be nice because my component system from '77 takes up the space of a refrigerator. Those new compact systems with tiny speakers put out a concert-hall sound and would leave more room for… well, there would be more room in the basement and then maybe I'd go down there more often to… well, it just seems like a new one would be really nice as long as it can also play cassette tapes.

And lest you think me self-centered, I haven't been thinking only about gifts I want. After all, it's better to give than to… not give. My son could use a new electric clock, since the clock at his place was wired in when the house was new in '52. You just know that baby could go bad any day. A couple new light fixtures would be perfect for my daughter, because I don't think they even make bulbs anymore for her vintage yard lights. And a case or two of batteries would take care of the things the grandkids got for Christmas last year, which is better than getting them something they don't need, right?

Gift ideas for my wife, on the other hand, are nearly impossible, because I've been buying her Christmas, birthday and Mother's Day presents for a long time now. It was already getting difficult to come up with practical gift ideas for her when we were dating in our teens. That reminds me of the worst gift I ever got her: a pink-and-white, rubber-backed, shag throw rug for her room. Oh, it was a nice rug, but I could tell it was probably not what she needed when she unwrapped it. I thought she liked pink. Not only that, the rug didn't last very long, or at least I don't remember seeing it around. I asked her about that but she said she doesn't remember the rug or anything about it. Of course, that was a long time ago and it wasn't a fancy gift, but I still find the loss of memory strange from a woman who can remember the birth date of a second cousin she has seen twice in the last thirty years. Anyway, that's why I buy electric stuff now. It may only work for thirty or forty years, but it sure lasts better than that rug did.

With this in mind, be careful what you wish for in a Christmas gift because many things, like rugs, for example, aren't very durable. I should write a book about gift ideas and then use the book as a gift for those hard-to-buy-for folks. You know, kill two birds with one stone, so to speak. Not too sure how you-know-who would feel about getting one though. I've been thinking it's been a while since I bought her any tools, but I may just keep on thinking for a while. (Wasn't born yesterday, ya know.)

Randolph

My sister and "the boyfriend" (later to become "the brother-in-law") were both in college preparing for options beyond someday having to live on a farm on a dead-end road with me and my parents. I didn't take it personally. I could find other young people to talk to—someday. I was fourteen and would hang around as they did their homework into the night around our kitchen table. It was interesting to watch an animal being dissected or to learn something about Einstein's theory, but there was a time when "the boyfriend" shared with me a writing project that made a lasting impression. It was titled "Randolph, the Rude-Nosed Dead Rear."

I thought to myself, *Can he do that? It doesn't even make sense.* The title was more than a little irreverent, but it struck me as humorous for the fact that it poked fun at a holiday icon. Thinking back, it exposed, maybe for the first time, that at least a small part of my personality was a bit irreverent as well. To this day I tend to "walk the other way" when someone suggests conformity to another's idea of right or wrong, their hero, or idea of success, or how some things should be done. I truly appreciate opinions, learning and the experience of others, but as an adult, conformity for conformity's sake—not so much. I'd rather think for myself. I've long been proud of Minnesota for a history of voting both Democratic and Republican, which indicates some independent thinking. And the irreverence for flawed systems from people like Rosa Parks, Teddy Roosevelt and August Landmesser are lessons not lost on me.

Irreverence also demands that I not take myself or others too seriously, on the basis that each of us is a little dysfunctional in one way or another. We all have faults—some of us just haven't been discovered yet. Families, communities, businesses and countries are not immune either. Nothing is perfect. So, as we go along responding to the environment around us, it seems a discerning eye should be accompanied by a little bit of humility. Indeed, one of the best definitions of a "friend" is: "a person who chooses to overlook your faults."

But it's the lighter side of irreverence I like best. It's an important tool for comedians, and there's nothing like a good ribbing as glue for a friendship. And marriage? With that much togetherness, if you don't learn to laugh with, or laugh at, each other once in a while, you're in for a rough ride, sweetheart.

I'm not a gifted writer and for years hesitated to "go public," fearing others would discover what I am or am not.

And I don't even remember what the Randolph story was about anymore, but Randolph the Rude-Nosed Dead Rear revealed a part of my personality that doesn't care if I'm not always taken seriously. Now I share because it's fun and that's good enough. It would be even better to always be right, but I had to start somewhere.

All this said, irreverence is just one part of a personality, personality being a combination of what you're born with and things you've experienced. Maybe your personality is defined more by optimism or sensitivity or ambition or something else. No doubt, some may think this topic interesting while others wonder, "What is this guy talking about?" Whatever the case, the variety you bring to the table is a healthy spice of life. Thank you to readers for your tolerance of some irreverence and shaky grammar shared here in this column over the last year. And know that I very much appreciate personalities different than mine. It makes great material. Keep up the good work!

Firewood

It's January, a time that tests firewood supplies and purifies the northland of piranhas, geckos, tarantulas, boa constrictors and other exotic pets that have either escaped or were let free by their loving, arguably insane, owners. And if you feed birds, you've probably noticed that the number of pet parakeets at the feeder is dwindling as fast as your firewood. Putting up firewood is a tradition at our home and when the kids were old enough, rather than allowing them to have a wallaby or some other exotic pet, we'd keep them busy by having them help with the firewood. Nothing against poisonous vipers, but they have their place.

The kids were good workers. They'd throw hay bales at their grandpa's farm, help pick up around the house, did their homework without too much badgering and as they got older they worked summer jobs. But for some reason, putting up firewood brought out a surly side in them and it would always go the same way. The day would start out fine, but before long, nitpicking would begin. "That's my piece." "Is that all you are going to carry?" "Dad, Dave called me a name!" "Mom, Beth took my piece of wood!" "Pat's not working."

After a while, every manner of excuse would be conjured up as to why production should come to a halt altogether. "My head hurts." "I'm tired." "Can't we do this tomorrow?" "My friends don't have to put up firewood." "This is stupid." "Pat's not working so I won't either." These complaints would go on for maybe a load or two, but we knew the day was coming to an end when wood started to "speed up." Let me explain.

Our system was to load the truck with wood, then unload it near the house using the kids' playground slide to send the pieces though the basement window to be piled as they came in. Proper protocol required a piece of wood be placed on the slide and gently sent down to our waiting arms—timing, obviously, being critical. But since I wasn't outside to keep "the game" under control, nitpicking and complaining blossomed into full-blown arguments that resulted in angry five-pound pieces of firewood shooting down the slide, leaving my wife and I feeling like we were participating in a high-stakes game of dodgeball.

"OKAY! THAT'S ENOUGH! I'VE HAD IT!" I'd yell from the basement. "WE'LL FINISH THE WOOD OURSELVES!" And just like that, the kids were off. Later, after finishing and having put things away, we'd come back in the house, by which time the kids had settled down and were playing happily together again. It's possible we were duped, but I was willing to cut them some slack since we hadn't allowed them a pet tiger or things of that nature.

I mention tigers because it was at about that time when, while on the job, I unwittingly walked up within a few yards of a Bengal tiger leashed to a spruce tree alongside a home within a mile of Cook. The tiger was staring back at me like I was a raw pork chop, which is a vision that will stay with me forever. Now, it's easy enough to reason that a tarantula or boa constrictor will not do well in –20° temps, but it bothered me to think that a runaway pet tiger could survive the Minnesota cold as long as it could find something to eat. That is a problem for us cross-country skiers. Maybe I'm oversensitive, but I was glad when a new law made it illegal to own tigers and the like in Minnesota. Nothing against Bengal tigers but I think that was a good call, and you can still go to Wisconsin or North Dakota if you really want to have one.

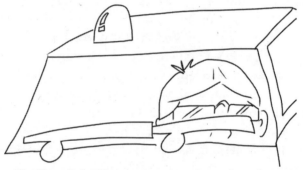

It Could Happen to Anybody

I wouldn't argue that my career was exemplary, stellar or even better than average, but I did my share for nearly thirty-nine years. So, when I visit with former workmates, it irks me a bit when the first thing they have to offer is "Remember that time you died?" or "Did you ever find that water heater?" And of course, I always have to remind the interrogator of the day, "No, I didn't die, actually," and "Yes, smarty pants, I did find the water heater… eventually." Then they'll say, "Oh, ha ha! That was rich! We still talk about it! You sure came up with some real—" And that's about the time I change the subject.

A reputation is important and it's something we build on

throughout life, right up to this very moment. To rid myself of these continued "burrs in the shorts," if you will, from my past, we'll set the record straight right here. The goal: leave behind, once and for all, these silly events that could have happened to anybody.

The first incident occurred decades ago on a work day in the countryside where several home visits were scheduled. It was noon, so I pulled off the road onto an abandoned drive way for lunch. Finishing a sandwich, I leaned back in the seat, closed my eyes and listened to the Paul Harvey radio show. At the end of the broadcast, I got back on the road and headed for my next stop. After a few minutes, a call came over the two-way radio. "Calling Truck Twenty-one." "Yes, this is Truck Twenty-one." "Are you all right?" "Ahhh… yes, I am. I'm heading south on Highway 53 for my next stop." "Okay, Twenty-one. We'll see you back at the shop when you get here. Chuckle, snicker."

Walking back to dispatch at the end of the day, I met a menacing pack of smiling scoundrels, jackals and nogoodniks waiting to greet me. One of them (his name is Greg Snyder) blurted out, "You're still alive!" "Huh? What are you talking about?" I snarled back. It turns out that while listening to Paul Harvey, a passing good Samaritan stopped to see if I needed help. As she approached the truck she saw me resting there, noticed the pop can on the dash and she simply walked away, assuming I was on lunch break, and she was correct. But after leaving, she second-guessed herself and thought, What if there was something wrong? So, as good Samaritans will do, she called the office to report that a fellow in Truck Twenty-one might be in distress—maybe dead. (You know, the world needs more good Samaritans, but I release them to help others for now on because I've had my turn.) Over the next few days, every person on the force with the exception of our general manager came to ask me if I was all right or still alive, but I know and you know that they knew that I was just fine. It was a long week.

A year or two later, I was to deliver an expensive, prototype water heater that was to be installed near Cook. I couldn't find rope so I used tape (really heavy, good tape) to secure the load and in addition, pushed other items in the truck box up against it to hold it firm. I left Virginia for Cook. The tape did not hold. I looked in the rearview mirror and watched the water heater going down Highway 53 at sixty miles per hour all by itself. Later I found the water heater back in the woods, and it didn't look like it did when it left the garage. It looked... rough. It could happen to anybody. End of story right? No. Greg found out what happened and he thought it was funny and told everybody at work about it, except for maybe the general manager. Now I can take a good ribbing as well as the next guy. Ha. Ha. But can we put this to rest?

Snowshoes

I suffered a catastrophic frame break at the master cord while snowshoeing a few weeks ago. A break at the master cord is a deep fear we wilderness snowshoe trekkers harbor because when you traverse the edge alone, potential danger is never far away. Fortunately, I wasn't traveling fast when the break occurred, which allowed time to safely come to a stop on the twisting trail through dark, tangled evergreens. However, I was 700 rods from camp with no shelter for an overnight stay, temps in the single digits and little time before nightfall to hunt for food or build life-sustaining fire. I pondered my predicament carefully, knowing the native peoples, explorers and trappers who came before me could face disaster with one wrong step.

You see, that's the way it is for today's wilderness trekkers—we don't actually see a lot of disaster nowadays so we have to settle for drama. Given this, no event is too dangerous, no mishap too small, no comment too insightful and no tuna sandwich or cell phone in our backpacks we want to talk about. Thirty minutes later I reached the welcome respite of our hunting camp just minutes before darkness and the overt dangers it brings, thankful once again for having survived to tell the story. Other than almost getting sweaty, it was no big deal. But like I said, we like drama.

I may have missed my time in history by 100 years or more, since I sometimes wish I had been a trapper. Back then, trappers did a lot of snowshoeing and they worked the woods and waters to make a respectable living. And unlike a mountain man, who often lived a Spartan life, this trapper would have come home every evening to a warm fire, a steaming hot meal and a happy family. I'm not a good trapper, so I had better wish also that accomplished trapper, Roger Waisanen of rural Cook, would be there to help and of course to skin out the furs because I'm not good at skinning furs either—I cut myself a lot.

If not a trapper, I would like to have been a farmer. Just as with trapping, back then one could make a decent living and it only need be a small spread with maybe ten cows, a couple horses, pigs, chickens and kids. It's hard work but satisfying at the end of the day. And if the plan worked out, I'd have the kids take over most of the operation of the farm once the oldest turned fifteen, which would allow me to do more snowshoeing and trapping on the side and of course, the taxes. I should probably think this through a bit more but you get the picture.

Regardless, snowshoeing in the here and now truly does inspire an appreciation for earlier days and simpler things: a nice trail, sunshine, fresh air and tracks in the snow. But it gets complicated when it comes time to purchase snowshoes, given the choices. There are traditional wood frame models such as Alaskan, Huron, Ojibwe or Bear Paw. Modern snowshoes incorporate aluminum, plastic or magnesium frames. Webbings can be combinations of rawhide, nylon, rubber and plastic. Bindings can have leather straps, buckles, snaps, rubber collars, ratchets and boot housings. Last and certainly not least, there is the issue of cost. From what I've been able to determine, there are snowshoes and there are expensive snowshoes. And as is usually the case, the expensive ones carry the prestige us wilderness trekkers like to flash on the rare occasions we meet other snowshoe trekkers in the parking lot. All this said, it was my wife's hope that I would not be taking out a loan for any new purchases this year, and that includes snowshoes.

Luckily, I have been able to borrow snowshoes from a couple friends and another pair from my son (all of whom should have known better) to help me decide which snowshoes I need, and that could take a while. Maybe even another season. But knowing that my next snowshoe purchase will be the best possible choice for my situation should make the expense more bearable for you-know-who. That's the "trap line" I'm currently working, anyway.

Bird Feeder Tactics

We put up our first bird feeder about a decade ago, join-
ing many others who feed birds over winter in exchange for
the color and activity they bring to a backyard. But it was apparent after a time that we weren't really feeding birds anymore—we were mostly feeding squirrels. I knew this because
squirrels with overstuffed cheeks loitered all day on, in and
under the feeder while anxious birds flittered about nearby. It
seemed a losing battle but we just kept throwing more seeds
at the issue and hoped for the best. Eventually, I figured I had
to do something about it.

First, I moved the feeder from the deck rail to a metal
pole. That didn't work. We tried greasing the pole. That didn't
work either. To limit the squirrels' intake, I blocked off half of
the Plexiglas window where the seeds were accessed. They
chewed a hole through the window to solve that issue. We
bought a new feeder and hung that in a tree. They chewed the
rope off and that feeder crashed to pieces. Finally, we bought
an even skinnier, taller pole, mounted a feeder on it and put it

in the middle of the yard, away from trees that might give the squirrels a tactical advantage. They climbed that pole faster than the first pole—grease or no grease.

Finally, I came to realize (albeit slowly) that if you want to feed birds you need to be at least smarter than a squirrel, or should I say squirrels, since we appear to have legions of them. So, this year, I took time to contemplate ways to squirrel-proof the bird feeder. An idea came—*why not put tin flashing on the pole so squirrels can't climb it?* It seemed too easy. After all, squirrels (my squirrels, anyway) seem to be able to scale plate glass windows and defy gravity. Some little piece of tin couldn't possibly stop them, could it? I cut a piece of tin with a hole in the middle and put it on the pole about four feet up. It works great! Finally, we have a feeder where the birds can eat freely, and whatever seeds they drop on the ground the squirrels are more than welcome to clean up! It's a win-win.

If you enjoy feeding birds, you probably had this figured out long ago, and if you enjoy feeding squirrels, this whole episode comes across as a lot to do about nothing. It's not that I don't like squirrels, since they're fun to watch also (as long as they're not chewing holes in my garage, tent, Duluth pack and bicycle seat), but I like to see chickadees enjoying a snack too. There is still one hiccup though. Since ending the red squirrels' monopoly on the feeder it appears we have yet another problem: flying squirrels. Not sure yet how to combat a nighttime aerial assault, but I've started thinking about it. At least now the birds have a chance at the seeds during daylight hours. Until I come up with a solution, we'll continue to throw more seeds at the issue. Good grief, squirrels couldn't have a Navy, too, could they?

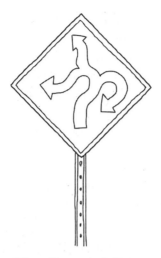

Maps, Trails and Directions

My dabbling in writing has been a journey without a map, so to speak, and it serves the practical purpose of filling in those occasional dull moments in retirement that fall between fishing, hiking, fixing, traveling, skiing, visiting, hunting, building, boating, shooting... volunteering... and cleaning. Sorry, we're going to have to slow down here—I'm almost sweating.

It was during one of those dull moments when I found myself reflecting about how my writing "trail" came to this point. I recalled a day at the job in 1978, when a few of us were having morning coffee while another, Phil Christianson, read a book at his desk, chuckling. After a bit, he started laughing out loud, which cued someone to ask, "What ya laughing about, Phil?" Collecting himself, Phil told us about the book he was reading by author Patrick McManus, which was a collection of zany predicaments McManus and his friends got themselves into during their younger years. So, Phil shared a few lines from the book and the next thing you know, the whole group of us laughed till we cried. Since then, I've read every book McManus has written. He's someone I relate to.

Later, I began following two syndicated columnists. The first was Sidney J. Harris, a deep thinker who passed away in 1986. He had a way of applying incredible insight to any topic at hand. Here are a few quotes: "There are always too many Democratic congressmen, too many Republican congressmen and never enough US congressmen." And, "The difference between patriotism and nationalism is that the patriot is proud of his country for what it does, and the nationalist is proud of his country no matter what it does; the first attitude creates responsibility, the second creates arrogance." And, "History repeats itself, but in such cunning disguise that we never detect the resemblance until the damage is done." His stuff is still relevant today. The other columnist, Dave Barry, was syndicated from 1983 to 2005. Not such a deep thinker, Dave admits he's still waiting to grow up, and his quotes include: "Camping is nature's way of promoting the motel business," and, "To an adolescent, there is nothing more embarrassing than a parent," and, "Skiing combines outdoor fun with knocking down trees with your face." It was a welcome dose of humor on an otherwise somber editorial page.

And while these writers influenced my life, we need to come back to Phil Christianson. Phil, who's retired and lives near Orr, amazed me with his array of knowledge. He's an avid reader and because he is a reader, he could offer interesting stories on interesting people. He could recite facts on all sorts of subjects and his insights were based on solid deduction from those facts. Trust me, if you want to debate Phil about something, do your homework first. In the months we worked together traveling from one job to another, I'd listen intently. It was time well spent, compared to unproductive debates of today grounded in television and radio soundbites, which are essentially merry-go-rounds—lots of motion, but they aren't going anywhere.

Indeed, Phil showed me how reading can be entertaining, provides interesting information and can even have you laughing out loud once in a while. It doesn't matter what trail you are on, those are good directions—especially for a writer.

Toys

I haven't done any road building in decades so it might surprise some folks to learn that I still own two dump trucks, a road grader and a front-end loader. But since my kids and grandkids had the chance to use the equipment, too, it seems it was worth the bother of keeping it around. After all, nobody makes toy road-building equipment like Tonka anymore, that's for sure.

It's possible I've given the impression that growing up on a dead-end road left me lacking, but other than the nonexistence of kids nearby, I had most everything I needed, including toys. Toys in my earliest youth were simple: blocks, a toy tool kit, a jack-in-the-box that scared the diapers off of me, a xylophone, a drum, a toy pistol (with real plastic pearl grips), Lincoln logs and my favorite, marbles. I also played with a set of Lennon Sisters paper dolls on occasion, but only because my sister made me do it.

Later, I collected baseball, football and World War II bubble gum cards, along with Hot Wheels cars, comic books, old coins, rocks and crystals. Then, when I was about fifteen or so, I thought I was too old for comic books and baseball cards so I packed up boxes of this stuff and sent it to the dump. The baseball card collection included several each of my favorite players, Mickey Mantle and Harmon Killebrew, which makes me cringe to think that perhaps my best chance at wealth is now soil in the old dump down near the river. All I have left is a 1960s-vintage NFL comic book with preseason rosters that lists retired Orr conservation officer Tom Fink as a member of the Minnesota Vikings. No offense to Tom, but if anybody has a Mickey Mantle or Harmon Killebrew card they want to trade for my Tom Fink comic book, I'm willing to deal. Anyway, after dropping comic books and collector cards I was finally old enough to buy a motorcycle. It wasn't a Harley, but it was the most treasured toy I ever had. Waiting for warm temperatures at this time of the year for the first ride was as anticipated as Christmas Eve was in the winter.

It was nice to enjoy toys when I did, because life speeds up in a hurry. Soon enough, a job, marriage and three beautiful babies came along, turning the few grown-up toys I owned into dust collectors. A short walk or bike ride was a luxury while we chased little ones around over the decade of the '80s, but thinking about that, the kids were more fun than toys, anyway, and unlike my early years on a dead-end road, I always had someone to play with.

Today I can afford more toys, and indeed I have purchased a few, but wouldn't you know it, grandkids are just as much fun as kids. We do many things together: fish, travel, hunt, celebrate birthdays and play games, not the least of which is baseball in the backyard on a warm summer night. All you need for that is a whiffle ball and a bat, so again my toys collect some dust, but that's okay. And don't bother looking for easy pickings at the old dump down near the river, because this time I'm not throwing anything away.

Book Report

My New Year resolution for 2018 was to get a book published composed of articles from this column or, in the event that didn't happen, make fudge for the thirty-six people who have confessed to following the column more or less regularly. Well, it might surprise you (it certainly surprises me) that a draft manuscript is nearly complete, with 60,000 words and ninety-plus stories scrummed together in what seems to me, anyway, a reasonable fashion. I'll be forwarding the manuscript to a company that will inform me how wrong I am and provide a quote of costs for design and publishing recommendations and since I'm the kind of guy that can choke on "costs" the progress of the project is, let's say, modest.

The problem now, of course, is that deer season is occurring at the same time as the culmination of the manuscript and between the two, it's messing with my focus. It's difficult sitting in a deer stand for mind-numbing hours then later sit at a computer with numbed mind trying to be creative. And both activities include questions that need attention. What title should be used for the book? How warm do you dress for ten degrees? Should I self-publish? Which deer stand to-day—Fleeting Glimpse or Angry Beaver? A two-color cover or full-color cover? Where are my bullets? Where are my glasses? It's exhausting. Really, have you seen my glasses?

I've enjoyed working on the book, especially on bad weather days, but it's deer season now. A time for campfires, shack food, anticipation and time alone in a dark forest. I'm sometimes spooked when alone in a dark forest but let's face it, with a .270 rifle in hand, I should have an edge. Opening morning this year provided nature's version of a Blue Angels flyover as six swans whooshed directly above my tree stand at sunrise. Later, I watched a pine marten chase a red squirrel and that evening, a robin-sized boreal owl landed on my stand giving me the most intense stare down I've ever been a part of. Deer? Didn't see one on opener but being immersed in nature always makes for a good day—as long as you stay warm.

My deer stands aren't very comfortable, or it's more accurate to say they aren't as comfortable as stands that have heat, music, hot food, reading material, spare blankets and Marvin windows. It's not that I wouldn't want a stand like that, it's just that "cost" thing again that gets me all choked up. For that kind of money, I'd prefer to build another garage. I'm hoping I won't need "that kind of money" to finish this book project, either, but that's a question for another day as having completed this, I'm heading back to the woods, my "free-air" deer stand, new snow and more adventures. That is my focus for now and as soon as deer season is over, I'll put all my energy back into the manuscript. That is, until ice fishing starts and let's face it—that looks to be soon. That's about all I have to say about the book. Hope you don't mind nuts in your fudge.

Observing Thanksgiving

Every year our family gathers in the fall to tell stories, eat turkey, share photos, hold babies, play with kids and watch football. This is pretty common stuff for a lot of families and while it may look like a din of confusion—kids running, people talking, nobody listening—it's all fairly predictable.

The biggest attraction, of course, is the football game, which draws a standing-room-only crowd in the living room, of which only two or three people actually watch the game and know the score. Under the guise of watching football, the event is a time to exchange all kinds of information. I learn quite a bit, actually. The price for beaver pelts is ridiculously low for another year. Irene explained how to can tomatoes, which I will forget by next fall. Justin covered corrective driving techniques on iced roads and Jeff reported there are no deer south of the Iron Range where he hunts, which covers a lot of ground, but I'll take his word for it.

It's great to have a doctor in the family now (which I was hoping could save me thousands), but wouldn't you know it, Kristina is a general practitioner and I need a surgeon. And doggone it, I forgot to ask Gary for advice on fixing my truck. Next year I'll make a list so this doesn't happen again. The living room crowd also happens to be a tough crowd at times known for good-natured barbs, but since this is predictable, most folks keep their comments pretty bland. You won't find anyone in the living room making a pitch for the federal budget or arguing who's the best quarterback in the NFL lest you become the center of attention. A fear I've had is that one of these years someone will make fun of our TV, which happens to be barely larger than a door on a microwave. I can imagine someday someone (probably my brother-in-law Al) will say:

"Hey, Leo, why don't you break open your crusty wallet and get yourself a real TV one of these days?" And then I'd have to say, "I'd love to, Al, but if you knew what I was getting paid for writing, you'd understand that I can't afford it."

And the kids are wonderful things. One, a quiet little dodger named Briar, can kick a balloon all day long. Dylan, Olivia and I were log rolling with a round footrest and we kind of broke it, but luckily for us nobody noticed. I still can't tell which twin is Nora and which is Leatah, so I simply didn't bother with formal introductions. And the baby didn't cry while I held her, which makes holding a baby most pleasant.

If I were to be a kitchen appliance, I always thought I'd want to be the refrigerator, but I've changed my mind. I'd rather be a dishwasher. Dishwashers, in our family, anyway, are revered. Last Thanksgiving, I made the mistake of sharing a disparaging comment about dishwashers and I was verbally gang-thrashed (the kitchen crowd, you see, is as tough as the living room crowd). So, this year, when I made an effort to begin washing some dishes after the meal, a mob showed up to study, load, caress and laud heaps of praise yet again upon my wonderful dishwasher, all but ignoring my valiant efforts at being helpful. If these people would treat me like they treat my dishwasher, I'd insist on being "the dishwasher" every year and throw in acting as the trash compactor for good measure. And while the crowd continued to gather at the dishwasher, I thought it would have been a good idea to break up duties, you know, have Mary wash windows, have Meg vacuum, have Garrett (a tall one) dust light fixtures and have Gail make the lip-curling coffee she's famous for but no, everyone was huddled around the dishwasher. After the commotion my dishwasher comment caused last year, I wasn't about to make any more proclamations in the kitchen. Except about the ladle. We didn't have a ladle for the gravy, which is a big deal for those of us who love gravy, so I went against my better judgment and proclaimed, "We could use a ladle for gravy." The comeback to that zinger was, "You sure have a lot to say about ladles for a guy who had nothing to do with any other part of preparing the meal." The comeback (by my wife, the budding comedian) got rave reviews from the kitchen crowd. That's about all I observed at Thanksgiving this year. The food was fantastic as always, by the way, and I hope you had a great Thanksgiving, too, even if it was as predictable as ours.

At the Table

When I was a kid, two of the closest neighbors on our dead-end road were Nestor and Amanda Vainio. Both were born a decade and some after the Civil War, putting them in their twenties when the Wright Brothers were gaining fame for flight, and they were retirement age when the television came to be. So, given they were eighty-something when I was eight-something, you wouldn't think we'd have much in common. Time, however, has something to say about that.

My memories of Nestor and Amanda begin at their kitchen table, where my mother would give Nestor a haircut while I sat happily nearby within reach of sugar cubes and pink mints. Their sturdy, two-story home was nestled in a grove of stately pines and heated largely by the wood-burning cook stove, which was regularly stoked, keeping the kitchen a cozy 75° at my head and a brisk 40° at my feet on cold winter days. Later, we'd move from the kitchen to the parlor, where the television was, in order to continue our visit, but if there was any information to be exchanged about people or personal matters, Mrs. Vainio would pause the discussion to turn off the television—she suspected Walter Cronkite could over-hear us. Their farm, with its rolling fields and interspersed woodlots, had been one of the finest in the township, with a beautiful garden and a classic barn overlooking the mean-dering Sturgeon River. And more often than not, when we'd drive past their place, if the two were not tending their gar-den, Mr. Vainio could be seen in the woods along the road trimming trees, clearing fallen debris, removing brush and piling refuse. He did this all by hand, of course, making his woods look like a park, but *What a lonely, endless toil* I thought to myself, feeling sorry for ol' Nestor. Over fifty years later, I can still envision him working in that woods along the road with his deeply set eyes and weathered face looking over to acknowledge me as I drive by. But I think I understand now.

Lately, I've taken to an almost daily habit of walking in the woods with hatchet in hand slowly picking my way through the forest scanning for tracks, thinking about the habitat and plans to improve it while enjoying the exercise. Maybe an old balsam could be dropped for low cover or a small stand of poplar harvested to provide for a new food source or maybe a trail removed to give animals more quiet space. One day, my choice of wear proved both cool enough and warm enough to have me perfectly comfortable for a survey that took me a half-mile deep in the woods. Soon enough, a darkening, over-cast sky predicted evening would come quickly and I had best head back. A pause during the trek to study a track (probably bobcat) found me curiously self-aware of my contentment. It dawned on me there was nothing else I would rather have been doing and it exposed, oddly enough, an uneasy aware-ness of mortality. I wanted this moment and more like it to continue—for a long time. It was a "thing."

Now, some may think me a bit daft for wandering about the forest day after day with little to show for the effort, but let them speculate. I find peace there. Since that "thing" in the woods, I've thought of Nestor Vainio, a man who lived off the fruits his land provided: food and income from the field, building materials and wood heat from the forest. I know now the last couple decades of his life clearing his woods were more than just laboriously passing time. I believe he appreciated the land more than we can ever know. And he genuinely enjoyed himself, with scythe in hand and an accompaniment of noisy jays who would steal his treats and squirrels that busied themselves in the protection of his presence. He was alone and comfortable with his thoughts, no longer committed to those complex things that speed our lives away and, apparently, or at least hopefully, he too was at peace. Maybe he had a "thing" as well.

In the book Walden, treasured American author Henry David Thoreau said this of his move to remote country and the simplicity it holds: "I went to the woods because I wished to live deliberately, to front only the essential facts of life, and see if I could not learn what it had to teach, and not, when I came to die, discover that I had not lived." Henry was a half century older than Nestor and Nestor had nearly a century on me but had we the chance to share coffee around the Vainios' table today, I think we would just go on and on about things. I think we'd see things eye to eye. We each enjoyed living on a dead-end road and spending time afield, which to our way of thinking, was in the middle of everything while in the middle of nothing at all.

See you later.

—Leo